M000272211

Custer's Strategy of Defeat

By
Chris Hoffert with Frederic C. Wagner III

With additional research from
Scott Lundin, Dale Kosman, George Kush, Michael Donahue, and Gerry Schultz

www.strategyofdefeat.com

Additional works by Christopher A. Hoffert

Contested Ground, the Story of the Little Bighorn Battle

Documentary produced in association with Ranger Steve Adelson's best-selling book 'Little Bighorn, Voices from a Distant Wind' and follows Steve's internationally renown telling of the battle and available from San Juan Publishing Group, Inc.

Official Selection at the Covellite International Film Festival 2016.

The Big Muddy Western Series

A five part western film series set in the early 1890s in Montana and follows a family as they brave a land of bandits, highway robbery, Indians, and fabled treasure.

Winner 'Best Narrative Fiction' at the Magic City Shorts Film Festival 2015.

Official Selection NXT Up Fest Film Festival 2017.

Praise for Custer's Strategy of Defeat

"This is a story that deserves to be told, and a fresh portrayal in film is long overdue. Major kudos for taking this on!"

- Mr. Ryan Trainor

"Chris did a fantastic job on the documentary "Contested Ground" which I wrote and produced. His cinematic talents are exceptional."

- Steve Adelson, LBH Battlefield National Monument Author & Historian

"Very, VERY well done!!! A damn sight better than anything you'll see in the movies."

- Frederic C. Wagner III, award winning author and Little Big Horn historian

"...this is going to be stunning. From the look of (the) artifact overlays, you're going to cover all the aspects, not just (Last Stand Hill)."

- Skye Milliman

"This looks like a work of passion. From the preview clips reminds me of Gettysburg. Well done Sir."

- Kenneth Goheen

Copyright 2021 by Christopher A. Hoffert.

All Rights Reserved.

No part of this book including, but not limited to: text, images, cover art, references, and citations, may be reproduced for any reason by any means whatsoever including any method of photographic or digital reproduction without the permission of the publisher.

Portions of this book may be used for research and/or educational purposed with permission, please query the publisher.

First Edition.

Printed in the United States.

WGA registration number:1990956
ISBN: 978-1-6485895-5-3

The Book Patch, LLC.
4400 Scottsdale Road, Scottsdale AZ, 85251
Https://www.thebookpatch.com/

Cover image: *Custer's Strategy of Defeat* featuring images of Gary Stewart and Trace Baukol filmed by Chris Hoffert and Robert DelTour.

Back cover: features footage stills from *Custer's Strategy of Defeat* of Ronald Glasgow, Gary Stewart, Matthew Yetter, Brandon Lewis, Henry Young Reed Jr., And Kyle C. Reed filmed by Robert DelTour, Jacqueline Lehr, and Heather Flynn.

Book and cover design, Christopher A. Hoffert.

This book is dedicated to the memory of Thomas R. Eastman (September 23, 1947 to December 27, 2020), without you, none of this would have been possible, and to all those who sacrificed, fought, and perished during the dark period of U.S. history known as "the Indian Wars."

In memoriam to a beloved friend to the Hoffert Family - Helori Graff.

In memoriam to a historian, researcher, producer, and friend to many - Steve Peckel.

In memoriam to a historian, researcher, and close friend - Gerry Schultz.

Table of Contents

Foreword

In 2012 historian Michael O'Keefe had his marvelous panoply of George Armstrong Custer and the battle of the Little Big Horn titles—books, articles, and anything else ever put into print, titles pushing some ten thousand in number, including the 1991 television mini-series, *Son of the Morning Star*—published by The Arthur H. Clark Company, at the time, an imprint of the University of Oklahoma Press. O'Keefe titled this two-volume set simply, *Custer, the Seventh Cavalry, and the Little Big Horn: A Bibliography*. Like all bibliographies, however, the next publication about the battle or the man—whether article or book—rendered everything before it, if not obsolete, then already incomplete. This 1991 TV mini-series adapted from the Evan Connell book of the same name—noted in O'Keefe's work—was the last and most clearly authentic video depiction ever put to film of the famous June 25, 1876 battle in the Montana Territory, Errol Flynn, John Wayne, and Dustin Hoffman notwithstanding. And now, some thirty years later, that movie—like O'Keefe's fine collection of titles—has been superseded, its originality made obsolete and debatable by Chris Hoffert's *Custer's Strategy of Defeat*.

While not the usual big-budget docudrama or Hollywood extravaganza, Hoffert's film has brought together an extremely talented group of filmmakers, combined with truly dedicated and masterful re-enactors, some of whom travel the country putting on dramatic reproductions of famous battle scenes, and uniform and equipment demonstrations. Cleverly using all sorts of modern filmmaking techniques, Hoffert has assembled a remarkable visual overview of events leading to, into, and through the battle of the Little Big Horn. The drama evoked in some of his long-range scenes is stunning, the vastness of the land, and the compact and undulating masses of troops and horses, worthy of dread were you a lone Indian scout watching the troops move toward their unsuspecting foe. His knowledge of the various and detailed events has enabled Hoffert to use terrain without exaggeration or questionable features so the viewer is transported back to the battle as one would believe it transpired. Even his use of spacing techniques, especially among individuals, gives us a realism we have not seen in larger, big-budget movies or documentaries.

In addition, the attention to detail—even the minutest things with the reenactors' uniforms—is truly extraordinary; details never before considered important, too picayune to be considered worthwhile, but details now demanding credibility and authenticity to make the effort real, combining to send the viewer back more than one hundred forty years.

In all this, Hoffert was assisted ably by re-enacting veterans such as Keith Herrin and men of his U. S. Cavalry School, along with the likes of Bill Rini (who portrays Captain Myles Keogh), Ronald Glasgow (an amazing "double" of George Custer's heroic adjutant, First Lieutenant William Winer Cooke), as well as descendants of men who actually fought in the battle: Greg Casteel (First Lieutenant Algernon Smith) and Jeff Reno (Major Marcus Reno), just to name a few.

No, *Custer's Strategy of Defeat* is not a Hollywood extravaganza, nor is it a twelve-hour documentary mini-series. What it is, is a truly authentic depiction of a monumental battle in the history of the American West, a battle, while paling in comparison to many of those fought subsequently across the world, but one with consequences lasting 'til this very day; a battle tolling the death knell of a peoples' way of life despite their trepidatious yet glorious victory; a battle of ignominy for a proud U. S. Army regiment. *Custer's Strategy of Defeat* is a film that brings the horror of a long-ago war's reality to our visual eyes as it really happened.

A very special thanks must go to the late-Tom Eastman who recently passed away. Tom portrayed the historian Walter Mason Camp and was a major force behind the making of this film. He was a good man, generous, kind, giving, understanding, gracious, and with an overriding desire for perfection and a never-quit personality that drove everyone forward. He shall be missed by everyone, and especially by those he loved and who loved him. Rest in peace Tom.

Frederic C. Wagner III
Pleasantville, New York
December 30, 2020

The U.S. Cavalry School

Custer's Strategy of Defeat was a tremendous undertaking for all involved; from the film crew to the actors, as well as the U.S. Cavalry School cadre, staff, and students--it was a labor with great respect for the history. There have been many filmings of Custer's Last Stand for television, documentaries, and movies over the years; but having this film project during the U.S. Cavalry School's Custer's Last Ride course and Little Bighorn reenactment was the best way to accomplish the scale envisioned by Chris Hoffert. To make a full docudrama on the Little Bighorn Battlefield using reenactors with this level of detail has never been done before. It was an honor for all to be part of this project.

The U.S. Cavalry School's Custer's Last Ride 8-day adventure is a step back into the past where students and cadre live the life of cavalry troopers on the Western Frontier with over eight days of history, tactics, horsemanship, and Native American studies. As in 1876, the school enlists troopers from across the world with varied riding skills from new to expert. You wear reproductions of the uniform and equipment the 7th Cavalry used during the campaign of 1876. You shoot the Army Single Action 45 Long Colt pistol and 1873 Springfield Trapdoor carbines. You cross the Little Bighorn River to conduct platoon and company tasks and missions daily, capture Native pony herds on the prairie, possibly ride in the once a year mounted ceremony on National Park's Last Stand Hill, and much more. You also learn horsemanship skills of the period with modern safety lessons and ride over large portions of the battlefield experiencing the Little Bighorn Battle like no other event.

Filming was a challenge. The weather was a huge obstacle and frequently caused delays to include canceling some of the reenactment days. Cavalry training for students and actors was modified with historical lectures and hands-on training during the hardest weather days. Many hours and scenes worked by crew and volunteers had to be completed between rainstorms, and everyone did a fantastic job going above and beyond.

Our cadre and staff did a phenomenal job of outfitting extras with uniforms and native attire options, equipment, and firearms, as well as feeding film crew and actors.

The School's Cadre and students are very excited to see everyone's hard work become part of Custer and Little Bighorn history. We hope that all get the chance to experience the history that we so enjoy living. Enlist with the U.S. Cavalry now at www.uscavalryschool.com.

Michael K Herrin
US Cavalry School
Ft Harrison, MT
January 12, 2021

Acknowledgements

So many have played a role in creating *Custer's Strategy of Defeat*, that to name them all would require a book in itself.

First and foremost, I must thank the cast and crew who sweated and bled during long hours on location to get the imagery "in the can." Without you, none of this would have been possible.

Special thanks are owed to Gerald Penn Jr, Keith Herrin, Buff C. Peters, Stan Smith, Mike Sullivan, Keith McGill, and the dozens of wonderful folks who backed our Kickstarter campaign. You all collectively provided the financial means for the creation of the film. Additionally, this thank you is extended to producers Thomas R. Eastman, Helori Graff, and Steve Peckel, who sadly are no longer with us. Your friendship and support will be greatly missed.

To the authors, historians, and researchers who selflessly assisted me in this film's research and its writing: Frederic C. Wagner III, Scott Lundin, Dale Kosman, George Kush, Michael Donahue, and Gerry Schultz, to name a few, thank you, not only for your endless knowledge on this subject but for your kind words of encouragement and support through this endeavor.

Last but not least, thank you to my family who put up with my obsession for all things Little Big Horn and the countless hours I spend behind the scenes doing my film work. If not for your love and support, I firmly believe that I would not be where I am today.

Christopher A. Hoffert
Writer, director, and editor
Custer's Strategy of Defeat

Preface

On the morning of June 25, 1876, famed Civil War General George Armstrong Custer made a fateful decision ending in a defeat that resulted in the death of 268 members of the 7th Cavalry and over 60 Sioux and Cheyenne warriors now romanticized as "Custer's Last Stand." This two-day battle marked a climax of cultural warfare spanning three decades of conflict between white expansionism and Native Americans desperately clinging to their way of life. The subsequent years saw the placement of hundreds of white and maroon marble and granite headstones along the lonely desolate hills and valley of the Little Big Horn, indicating where men fell in battle.

There is hardly another battle in history that creates so much debate and discussion as this one. The ambiguity and mystery of the event bred myths and legends that now transcend time. The purpose of this book and film is not an "end all, be all" in terms of the entire story--this battle is far to complex for just a two-hour movie, but it will be a comprehensive telling of the significant elements of those two bloody days in 1876, as told by those who survived.

Many of the documentaries, movies, and television dramas made about this battle, all beat a similar drum--focusing on the myths, legends, lore, and conjecture. It is the goal of all those involved in this project not to follow this trope because it does a disservice to the continued study of history. In keeping with this promise, *Custer's Strategy of Defeat* leans heavily on firsthand accounts, archaeology, and as much corroborating evidence as possible to tell the story you are about to read.

Like the events leading up to the real battle, *Custer's Strategy of Defeat* is a culmination of events in itself. The film's foundation was laid over three years before the cast and crew stepped foot on the hallowed ground of the battlefield in 2019. Chris Hoffert; the film's writer, director, and editor; began networking and pitching an idea about doing something fresh and different on the battle about a year after producing the short documentary *Contested Ground* for Steve Adelson's book *Little Bighorn, Voices from a Distant Wind* in 2016.

He networked with various authors, historians, reenactors, and producers until all the elements needed for a quality visual telling of the battle were in place.

Custer's Strategy of Defeat took three years of networking, writing, and fundraising to build a budget and script; 14 long and grueling days to capture the imagery, and two years to edit the film and create the audiovisual elements that bring the story to life. The passion for good storytelling and dedication to creating an accurate visual depiction of history is evident in the thousands of hours so many have poured into making this film. While perfectly imperfect, this movie is the *Son of the Morning Star* for the modern generation. This film incorporates as much of the battle's current known history and filters out as much of the conjecture and myths as possible. It is a gritty "boots on the ground" exploration of the entire fight and its participants.

Without further adieu, *Custer's Strategy of Defeat.*

The Screenplay

DEDICATION TITLE 1:
The following film is dedicated to the loving memory of Thomas R. Eastman, 1947 to 2020.

FADE IN:

PROLOGUE TITLE 1:
Tension between the United States and the Lakota escalated in 1874 when Lt. Col. George Armstrong Custer was ordered to explore the Black Hills, a violation of the Treaty of Fort Laramie.

PROLOGUE TITLE 2:
During the expedition, gold was discovered.

PROLOGUE TITLE 3:
The United States tried negotiating with the Lakota to purchase the Black Hills, but the offer was rejected.

PROLOGUE TITLE 4:
The climax came in the winter of 1875 when the Commissioner of Indian Affairs issued an ultimatum requiring all Sioux report to a reservation by January 31st, 1876.

PROLOGUE TITLE 5:
The deadline came with virtually no response from the tribes, and the matter was turned over to the war department.

OPENING TITLE SEQUENCE:
Burning photos motif.

FADE TO BLACK.

FADE IN:

INT. TENT INTERVIEW - DAY

A canvas tent sits perched in the shade of some trees. A FIGURE enters with briefcase and places the stacked contents on an old wood desk.

> WALTER CAMP (V.O.)
> The Battle of the Little Big Horn is one of the most written about and debated battles in American history.

A HAND lays a map of the Little Big Horn battle across the table then places papers neatly stacked on the side with some pencils.

> WALTER CAMP (V.O.)
> It has come to be known as Custer's Last Stand,
> and it is steeped in myth, legends, and lore.

WALTER CAMP; fifties, fair skin, receding hair, researcher, eastern accent; grabs a pencil and sharpens it then lays it down gently on the map.

> WALTER CAMP (V.O.)
> My name is Walter Mason Camp.
>> (beat)
> In the early nineteen-hundreds, I began
> documenting the testimonies of the soldiers and
> Natives who fought this battle during the period
> known as the Indian Wars.

He takes out a notebook and turn pages past copious notes to the first available blank page.

> WALTER CAMP (V.O.)
> It is my sincere hope that this research will ignite a
> passion to keep the history alive...lest we forget.

He takes out a notebook and turn pages past copious notes to the first available blank page.

> WALTER CAMP (V.O.)
> This is the story as it was told to me.

A pencil is raised to the notebook. The hand scribbles, "Little Big Horn interviews, June, 1910."

> WALTER CAMP (V.O.)
> Little Big Horn interviews...June, nineteen-ten.

INT. TENT INTERVIEW DAY

Walter Camp looks up as OLD GODFREY enters and sits. Old Godfrey takes a few seconds to get comfortable as he adjusts his EARLY 1900S ATTIRE.

> WALTER CAMP
> Could you please state your name and your relation
> to the battle on June, eighteen seventy-six?

> OLD GODFREY
> Edward Settle Godfrey, Lieutenant, Seventh U.S.
> Cavalry. I was the commander of Company K.

Walter Camp writes in his notebook.

WALTER CAMP
Let's begin on the morning of June twenty-fifth,
eighteen seventy-six.

Old Godfrey's eyes look distant and his being seems to move across time as a sullen
expression falls over his face.

OLD GODFREY
We were riding on the Eastern side of the divide
of the Wolf Mountains. It was early, perhaps
breakfast time. We had marched all night.

CUT TO:

EXT. MOUNTAINS - MORNING

OLD GODFREY (V.O.)(CONTD)
Colonel Keogh reported a Sergeant had seen an
Indian gettin' hard bread from a box that had been
lost during the night.

Rough peaks accentuate a rolling drop of land on both sides of the Wolf Mountains.
In a depression surrounded by light trees, hundreds of SOLDIERS ride in formation.

LIEUTENANT EDWARD GODFREY; dark eyes, dark hair, bushy mustache; rides
at the head of many SOLDIERS.

Godfrey watches as SERGEANT WILLIAM CURTISS; 30 years old, brown eyes,
brown hair, dark complexion; rides past.

MAIN TITLE 2:
June 25th, 1876
Near Halt 2
7:00 A.M.

Curtiss rides up to CAPTAIN MYLES KEOGH; 36 years old, blue eyes, dark hair,
mustache with lip goatee; rides his horse COMANCHE. He surveys the terrain and
SOLDIERS riding.

CURTISS
Colonel Keogh, sir...

Curtiss salutes Keogh, Keogh returns the salutation.

CURTISS
Sergeant Curtiss, F company. I must report that on
our last halt some items came loose from the
saddle and were lost.

                              KEOGH
          Goddamnit!
                    (shoots harsh look)
          Take four soldiers. You will retrieve the items and
          report back to me with haste. I'll have to report
          this to Captain Yates.

Keogh turns his horse.

                              CURTISS
          Sir--

Keogh looks back.

                              CURTISS
          It was dark and we were hurried, my apologies.

                              KEOGH
          Just get the hell out of here!

                              CURTISS
          Yes sir.

Curtiss salutes, Keogh exits. Curtiss exits.

                              OLD GODFREY (V.O.)
          Myles Keogh was a tough one. He liked his drink
          and was quick with a tongue lashing.

INT. TENT INTERVIEW - DAY

Walter Camp's hand writes "Charles Varnum, Chief of Scouts."

OLD VARNUM now sits where Old Godfrey had been he watches Walter Camp
writing.

                              WALTER CAMP
          Mister Varnum, you were in charge of the scouts
          on the day of the battle?

                              OLD VARNUM
          Yes sir.

                              WALTER CAMP
          At what point did you see the Indian village, and
          what can you tell me about it?

15

OLD VARNUM

I had sent word to Custer that the Scouts reported
seeing a large village out in the valley. He came at
once to where I was.

EXT. MOUNTAIN PEAK - MORNING - CONTINUOUS

OLD VARNUM (V.O.)(CONTD)
We climbed the bluff and the Scouts tried to show
Custer what they saw...

A peak on the high point near the divide of the Wolf Mountains.

MAIN TITLE 3:
The Crow's Nest
8:00 A.M.

SECOND LIEUTENANT CHARLES VARNUM; dark hair, brown eyes, trimmed
dark mustache; struggles up a steep slope. He kneels and waits.

Four Crow SCOUTS; HALF YELLOW FACE, and WHITE MAN RUNS HIM; sit
smoking.

OLD VARNUM (V.O.)
The Scouts had been watchin' some Indians to our
front thinkin' we might get spotted.

MITCH BOUYER; half breed Indian, black eyes, black hair, dark skin; sits smoking
an elaborate pipe.

A small group of NATIVES ride near the divide and then disappear behind some trees.

Army scouts FRED GERARD, BLOODY KNIFE, CHARLEY REYNOLDS, enter
and move to the edge of the ridge and look into the valley.

G. Custer enters, his feet then kneels revealing his rugged face. Varnum hands G.
Custer a pair of binoculars.

VARNUM
General, they say the village is in the valley of the
Little Horn just there, about fifteen miles distant.
(he points)

G. Custer scans the distance with binoculars. A heavy "smog-like" layer hangs over
the valley, he sees nothing.

G. CUSTER
I can't see anything!

16

Varnum looks to the distance and back to G. Custer.

> VARNUM
>
> General, the scouts say they see a huge pony herd just to the western bluffs of the river valley bottom.

Custer looks more desperately--still nothing.

> VARNUM (CONT'D)
>
> They say it looks like worms in the grass.

G. Custer looks to Varnum who is still awaiting a reaction.

> CHARLEY REYNOLDS
>
> The village is there General.

> BOUYER
>
> (looks distant)
> If you don't find more Indians in that valley than you ever saw together before, you can hang me.

Bouyer looks to G. Custer who meets his gaze.

> G. CUSTER
>
> It would do a damned sight of good to hang you, wouldn't it?

Both stare at each other.

> HALF YELLOW FACE
>
> (in Crow)
> These Sioux have seen the smoke of our camp. We must attack now!

Gerard translates Crow to English for G. Custer.

> G. CUSTER
>
> This camp hasn't seen our army I want to wait until it is dark, and then we march.

Gerard translates English.

> WHITE MAN RUNS HIM
>
> (in Crow)
> That plan is no good, the Sioux have already spotted your soldiers.

> G. CUSTER
>
> We will wait, and we will attack tomorrow.

> RED STAR
> (in Crow)
> You must attack at once and capture the horses of
> the Sioux.

G. Custer turns Varnum.

> G. CUSTER
> Let's be on with it. Keep a few scouts out to the
> front at all times.

> VARNUM
> Yes sir!

ALL exit.

> OLD VARNUM (V.O.)
> We went down the hill and took four horses and
> rejoined the troops.

EXT. MOUNTAINS - MORNING - CONTINUOUS

MAIN TITLE 4:
Halt 2
Midmorning

Dozens of SOLDIERS are dismounted and relaxing for the first time in several hours. Curtiss and GROUP ride up.

> WALTER CAMP (V.O.)
> As the command settled in during the second halt,
> Sergeant Curtiss returned with pressing news.

CAPTAIN GEORGE YATES; 33 years old, dirty blonde hair, bushy dirty blonde mustache; stands with Keogh near several SOLDIERS.

> YATES
> (to Keogh)
> You're gonna have to put spurs to those damn
> mules. They're slowin' everything up.

> KEOGH
> Damn things are beat and those packers didn't
> tighten them loads well enough.

FIRST LIEUTENANT WILLIAM "W. W." COOKE; dark hair, brown eyes, mustache with "Dundreary" sideburns; stands smoking with LIEUTENANT JAMES CALHOUN, CAPTAIN TOM CUSTER, Godfrey, CAPTAIN MYLES MOYLAN, and LIEUTENANT WINFIELD EDGERLY.

18

ALL watch Curtiss ride up and dismount near Yates, Curtiss--winded, salutes.

                    CURTISS
          Captain Yates sir!

Yates turns.

                    CURTISS
          Sir, we have returned having secured all the items.

                    YATES
          Very well Sergeant, thank you.

Yates salutes.

                    CURTISS
          Sir--

                    YATES
          Yes?

Curtiss looks away momentarily in shame, then back.

                    CURTISS
          Well, sir...when we returned...we found several
          hostiles rifling through the field.

                    YATES
          How many hostiles?

                    CURTISS
          A few, I'm--I'm not sure. They skedaddled when
          we arrived.

                    YATES
          Ah hell! Carry on!

Yate's salutes, Curtiss exits.

Cooke approaches Yates.

                    COOKE
          Colonel Yates, what's the problem?

ALL eavesdrop.

                    YATES
               (upset)
          We lost a pack on the ride up.
               (MORE)

19

YATES (CONT'D)
I sent a Sergeant back and he found a damned
Indian going through a bread box. They chased
them off, but I fear we've been spotted.

COOKE
Damn. I'll report it to the General.

Both salute, Yates exits, Cooke returns to the group.

TOM CUSTER
I'll inform Autie.

COOKE
Ok.

Tom Custer exits.

COOKE
(to Edgerly)
I believe you'll have the chance to bathe your
maiden sabre today.

ALL LAUGH.

INT. TENT INTERVIEW - DAY

Walter Camp looks up to Old Godfrey.

WALTER CAMP
The command had been spotted?

OLD GODFREY
The Crow scouts had seen some Indians and
thought they had seen the dust of the command
and were aware of our presence in the country.

EXT. MOUNTAINS - MORNING - MOMENTS LATER

OLD GODFREY (V.O.)
Tom Custer went immediately to inform General
Custer what had been seen.

G. Custer stands with Varnum surrounded by several SCOUTS.

Tom Custer enters and stops.

TOM CUSTER
Autie!

G. Custer looks, motions Tom Custer to wait, then back to Varnum.

                    G. CUSTER
Are you able to continue scouting?

                    VARNUM
I have to ride anyway and one place is as good as
another.

                    G. CUSTER
Go ahead then.

Varnum salutes and exits.BLOODY KNIFE; copper complexion; looks uneasy. G.
Custer notices his friend's apprehension.

                    BLOODY KNIFE
          (in Crow)
Many Sioux.

                    G. CUSTER
          (in Crow)
I think we can get through them all in one day.

                    BLOODY KNIFE
          (in Crow)
You and I are both going home tonight by a road
we do not know.

Custer ignores the comment and walks to Tom Custer.

                    G. CUSTER
What is it Tom?

                    TOM CUSTER
Captain Yates reported his company lost a pack
back on the trail. He sent a detail to retrieve it and
encountered a small group of hostiles picking
through it.

                    G. CUSTER
What are you saying?

                    TOM CUSTER
It seems we've been spotted.

Custer's expression changes from professional calm to irritation.

                    G. CUSTER
Sound officer's call--now!

Tom Custer exits.

                         TOM CUSTER (O.S.)
           Sound Officer's Call!

A bugle BLOWS "Officer's Call" O.S.--the sound echoes through the hills.

Scout GEORGE HERENDEEN; late twenties, nondescript white male, ruddy,
weathered; spurs his horse and stops near G. Custer.

                         HERENDEEN
           General, I'm ready to take a message to General
           Terry down Tulloch's Fork.

Herendeen points down a long winding creek on the right. G. Custer looks then back
to Herendeen.

                         G. CUSTER
           There is no occasion for sending you there. The
           Indians are to our front and have since discovered
           us. That'll be all Mister Herendeen.

Both exit.

INT. TENT INTERVIEW - DAY

Old Godfrey sits waiting for Walter Camp to finish writing. Walter Camp looks up.

                         WALTER CAMP
           After learning of this, what actions did Custer take?

                         OLD GODFREY
           General Custer had officer's call sounded and we
           were informed what had happened.

EXT. MOUNTAINS - MORNING - MOMENTS LATER

                         OLD GODFREY (V.O.)
           The Scouts reported that the Sioux had discovered
           the command and concealment was useless.

MAIN TITLE 5:
Officer's call
9:20 A.M.

G. Custer reclines in front of a semi-circle of the OFFICERS under a lonely tree some
distance away from a group of soldiers.

                    G. CUSTER
Gentlemen, my plans were to hide our troops and
attack tomorrow, but it seems all hope of surprise
is now gone and the only way of catching the
Indians is to march at once.

Charley Reynolds locks eyes with G. Custer.

                    CHARLEY REYNOLDS
General, this is the biggest bunch of Indians I've
ever seen.

                    G. CUSTER
                (ignoring Reynolds)
The scouts report that there's a large village about
fifteen miles ahead in the valley of the Little Horn.
I am not yet convinced of its size, because I have
not seen it.

                    KEOGH
What of the reports of hostiles to our rear?

                    G. CUSTER
                (glares at Yates)
Earlier, Colonel Yates' company lost a pack on the
trail.

Yates looks down.

                    G. CUSTER (CONT'D)
On returning they found several hostiles going
through it--
                (glares over the whole group)
The scouts also report small bands of hostiles to
our front who are keeping watch on our
movements.

MAJOR MARCUS RENO; dark hair, dark eyes, ruddy face; looks up.

                    RENO
What are our orders?

                    G. CUSTER
Major Reno, I see no other option other than to
attack at once.

                    RENO
And what of Gen'l Terry?

G. CUSTER
(glares)
We can no longer afford to wait for General Terry.
The Indians will scatter and all will be for naught.
Does anyone object?

OFFICERS look to each other's left and right and then back to G. Custer.

G. CUSTER
Very well then, every company is to detail six
enlisted men and one non-commissioned officer to
help the mules along. Get the coffee-coolers up. I
will detail battalions after we cross the divide.

Benteen steps forward.

BENTEEN
Hadn't we better keep the regiment together,
General? If this village is as big as they say it is,
we'll need every man we have.

G. Custer glares at Benteen.

G. CUSTER
Colonel Benteen, you have your orders Benteen,
follow them!

Benteen scowls. G. Custer focuses to the group.

G. CUSTER (CONT'D)
Check your companies. Each man is to have one-
hundred rounds carbine and twenty-four Colt
rounds. The company commander who first
reports will have the advance.

G. Custer stands.

G. CUSTER
As you were gentlemen.

Godfrey watches.

ALL exit. Benteen glares at Custer now losing himself in thought.

INT. TENT INTERVIEW - DAY

>   OLD GODFREY
>   I thought I certainly would be of the advance, but
>   some company commanders reported without
>   seeing to anything, and so they got the lead.

Walter Camp scribbles feverishly in his notebook, stops, and looks up.

>   WALTER CAMP
>   Who was placed in charge of the pack train?

>   OLD GODFREY
>   McDougall was the last to report so he was given
>   the packs to escort that day.

Benteen looks to move then stops.

>   BENTEEN
>   H company is ready.

Custer is caught off guard and looks. OTHERS stop and look.

>   G. CUSTER
>   So be it Colonel. Your company will have the
>   advance.

Benteen smirks and exits.

INT. TENT INTERVIEW - DAY

Walter Camp looks up from his notes.

>   WALTER CAMP
>   Was it around this point that General Custer
>   divided his forces?

Old Godfrey nods.

>   OLD GODFREY
>   After passing the divide, Benteen received his
>   orders to make a scout to the left. I reported for
>   duty with his battalion.

EXT. ROLLING HILLS - MORNING - LATER

>   OLD GODFREY (V.O.)
>   Custer expected to find Indians scattered along the
>   river.

25

MAIN TITLE 7:
Dividing the command
11:00 A.M.

Benteen and a company of SOLDIERS march there horses forward, dust trailing from the rear.

Benteen sees G. Custer and Cooke approaching. He holds his hand up.

> BENTEEN
> Halt!

G. Custer and Cooke ride up. Benteen takes his hat off and wipes his brow with a neckerchief.

> G. CUSTER
> Colonel Benteen, I want you to proceed to that line of bluffs and pitch into anything you come across.

Benteen looks to the bluffs and then back to Custer.

> G. CUSTER (CONT'D)
> You will take your company along with French and Godfrey's companies. You'll need no scouts, this you'll do. Keep an advanced party of six soldiers and one officer ahead of your command.

> BENTEEN
> I'll take Weir's D company instead of M.

G. Custer's expression changes to acute anger.

> G. CUSTER
> (shouting)
> Colonel Benteen--

G. Custer pauses.

> G. CUSTER (CONT'D)
> (calmer tone)
> Well, damn it all to hell! Take D company.

Benteen salutes, G. Custer does not return it and rides off. Benteen smirks and waves his hand in a forward motion. ALL exit.

> WALTER CAMP (V.O.)
> Custer and Benteen's relationship was abrasive in all accords;
> (MORE)

26

                    WALTER CAMP (V.O.) (CONT'D)
        but nonetheless, Captain Benteen set out on what
        he later called 'valley hunting ad infinitum.'

                                        CROSSFADE:

EXT. ROLLING HILLS - MORNING - CONTINUOUS

Two-Hundred SOLDIERS move forward. G. Custer rides, his red tie blowing over
his shoulder--his face white and serious.

                    WALTER CAMP (V.O.)
        Custer and the regiment pressed on, the pieces of
        the pending fight slowly falling into place.

                                        CROSSFADE:

EXT. ROLLING HILLS - MORNING - MOMENTS LATER

G. Custer and GROUP ride up to Reno, Reno HALTS his formation.

                    G. CUSTER
        Major Reno, take companies A, G, and M and
        proceed down the left bank of the creek.

                    RENO
        It will be done.

Cooke exits.

                    G. CUSTER
        Voss!

Voss rides alongside G. Custer.

                    G. CUSTER
        Send a message to Benteen. If he finds nothing
        before reaching the first line of bluffs then to go to
        the second line with the same instructions.

                    VOSS
        Yes sir!

Voss salutes and rides off.

                    WALTER CAMP (V.O.)
        Will you please say your name and from which
        tribe you are from?

INT. TENT INTERVIEW - DAY

OLD HE DOG; 70 years old, Native American, weathered face, heavy accent sits in front of Walter Camp.

> OLD HE DOG
> He Dog, I Oglala Lakota Sioux tribe with Crazy Horse.

> WALTER CAMP
> What can you tell me of the Native camp?

> OLD HE DOG
> We moved to the Little Bighorn third day after Crook fight. Sioux did not want to fight and so when got away off at Little Bighorn thought would have no more fighting.

EXT. NATIVE VILLAGE MORNING - DAY

> OLD HE DOG (V.O.)
> We had our wives and children with us and had to get buffalo meat for them and wished to be let alone.

MAIN TITLE 5A:
Valley of the Little Big Horn
11:00 A.M.

HE DOG; dark eyes, dark hair, constant angry expression; watches.

Horse WHINNIES echo in the distance, He looks--a large pony herd moves about the plains. He looks back, NATIVE CHILDREN run and play and LAUGH. He smiles.

> OLD HE DOG (V.O.)
> Sitting Bull prayed for the safety of the Sioux.

EXT. HILL - MORNING - CONTINUOUS

SITTING BULL; Native American, forties, short, weathered face, dark hair, muscular frame; sits praying on a blanket a distance away from the village.

> SITTING BULL
> (in Sioux)
> Ho he leháŋl Wakáŋ Taŋká nišnála niwakaŋ,
> T'huŋkašila oyáte kiŋ ób óhiŋni uŋšimič'iya waúŋ
> čha makásitomniyaŋ namá'uŋ ye. Leháŋl oúŋ teča
> waŋ él itóheya uŋhínažiŋpi kiŋ čha uŋšíuŋlapi ye.
> (MORE)

SITTING BULL (CONT'D)
Wičhóuŋ wáwala waŋ na wóiyaksape waŋ uŋk'úpi
čhá wičhóuŋčhae íyókhihe kiŋ lé wótheika šni úŋpi
kté ló. Toná aíyapi na toná owótaŋla šni na toná
wičhóiye šikšíča úŋpi kin toéčhuŋ šikšíča kin lená
íuŋtókapi šni na ohókičhilapi čha óunkiyapi ye.
Wakáŋ Taŋká očháŋku kiŋ uŋkíyutaŋiŋpi ye. He lé
miyé Tatáŋka Íyotake.
(translation)
Ho Great Spirit you are the only one who is
sacred, Grandfather I always lived a simple life
with my people so here me! Now we are facing a
new way of life so have pity on us! Give us a
peaceful life and guidance so the next generations
will life with no hardship. Help us that those who
are gossip and those who are deceitful and those
who are using bad words that their bad doings will
not affect us and to respect each other. Great
Spirit show us the way! This is me Sitting Bull.

EXT. NATIVE VILLAGE - MORNING - CONTINUOUS

GALL; Native American, dark hair, two-hundred fifty pounds, gifted leader; sits
watching GALL CHILDREN 1, 2, & 3 run and play amongst several teepees.

GALL CHILD 1
(in Sioux)
Omáyaluspa oyákihi šni.
(translation)
You can't catch me, I'll get you!

He looks over to GALL WIVES 1 & 2. He smiles, they smile.

Young and old NATIVES sit around breakfast campfires. Nondescript DIALOGUE
fills the air.

EXT. RIVER - MORNING - CONTINUOUS

CRAZY HORSE; mixed Native American, small, dark hair, fair skinned, narrow face,
scar on left cheek; sits alone near the river in deep meditation.

The river ROARS to Crazy Horse's ears, drowning out everything else. Native
American war drums BEAT distant--heard only by him.

He opens his eyes, the water ripples in front of him.

29

> OLD HE DOG (V.O.)
> There were more Hunkpapa than any other tribe.
> Minneconju next, maybe eighteen-hundred lodges
> in whole village.

Thousands of teepees are grouped by tribe stretched along the length of the valley for as far as the eye can see.

EXT. RIVER - DAY - CONTINUOUS

MAIN TITLE 7:
The attack begins
Noon

Reno crosses a river and meets Cooke and Keogh. They salute.

> COOKE
> Major Reno, the village is just ahead and running
> away.

Reno looks to his front and distant.

> COOKE (CONT'D)
> General Custer wishes for you to move your
> companies forward at as rapid a gait as prudent
> and charge the village.

Reno looks back to Cooke.

> RENO
> Will the General be coming along?

Keogh subtly sneers at Reno's comment.

> COOKE
> Sir, you'll be supported by the whole command.

> RENO
> Understood.

Cooke and Reno shake hands. All exit.

> WALTER CAMP (V.O.)
> With the attack imminent, Reno pushed his scouts
> out ahead of the column.

INT. TENT - DAY

Words appear across the page of a notebook as Walter Camp compiles his thoughts feverishly.

> WALTER CAMP (V.O.)
> Far from the Indian camp, a warrior named Deeds
> was out hunting when Reno's scouts happened
> upon them.

EXT. TREES - DAY

DEEDS; dark eyes, black hair, Native American, Hunkpapa Lakota Sioux, teens; and STANDING BLACK BEAR through some brush near the river far from camp.

A pony drinks from the river, Deeds approaches slowly his hand raised in peace to the animal.

> WALTER CAMP (V.O.)
> This chance encounter saw the first shots of the
> battle being fired and the first casualty...Deeds.

Horse WHINNIES--the pony rears its head nervously. Deeds looks--SCOUTS emerge from the timber along the river. Deeds' eyes widen in fear.

> DEEDS
> (in Sioux)
> Milá háŋska! Úpelo! Ináni igláka po!
> (translation)
> Long Knifes! They are coming! Hurry move (the
> camp)!

Standing Black Bear retreats to his pony. Deeds tries to grab the pony--it bolts.

> STANDING BLACK BEAR
> (screaming in Sioux)
> Ógle toto kiŋ hená úpelo!
> (translation)
> The blue coats are coming!

The Scouts see Deeds and Standing Black Bear. The Scouts charge--Deeds flees.

> WALTER CAMP (V.O.)
> This chance encounter saw the first shots of the
> battle being fired and the first casualty...Deeds.

The Scouts ride him down--BANG! Deeds falls. His eyes fall upon a blue sky visage--final breath.

STANDING BLACK BEAR
(more distant)
(in Sioux)
Hená úpelo! Ogle toto! Hená úpelo!
(translation)
They are coming! The Blue Coats! They are coming!

His voice echoes around the valley. REE SCOUT looks up as Standing Black Bear disappears into the distant terrain.

INT. TENT INTERVIEW - DAY

OLD FOOLISH ELK; Native, 54 years old; sits across from Walter Camp.

WALTER CAMP
Was the village aware of Custer's approach?

OLD FOOLISH ELK
There was some kind of vague report that soldiers were coming, but we didn't know if it was Crook or Custer.

EXT. NATIVE VILLAGE - MORNING - MOMENTS LATER

WALTER CAMP (V.O.)
News of Reno's sighting reached Chief Gall at the southern end of the camp.

Standing Black Bear rides into the Hunkpapa Sioux camp at break neck speed.

STANDING BLACK BEAR
(in Sioux)
Akíčhita úpeló!
(translation)
The soldiers come!

Foolish Elk looks. Gall looks.

GALL
(motions to warriors nearby)
(in Sioux)
Šúŋkawakáŋ hená gliyóya po!
(translation)
Get the ponies!

STANDING BLACK BEAR
(in Sioux)
Čhetáŋ Wečhá ktepi.
(MORE)

                    STANDING BLACK BEAR (CONT'D)
          (translation)
     They killed Lone Hawk (Deeds).

Gall approaches Standing Black Bear.

                         GALL
          (in Sioux)
     hwo?
          (translation)
     Where are they?

Standing Black Bear points to the south.

                    STANDING BLACK BEAR
          (in Sioux)
     Kákhiya wakpá ikhíyela yápi.
          (translation)
     Over there, they went near the river.

Gall turns to Gall Wives 1 & 2 and GALL Children 1, 2, & 3.

                         GALL
          (in Sioux)
     Wóyuha gluwítaya naháŋ iyáya po!
     Átawičhauŋyapi kteló.
          (translation)
     Gather your things and run. We'll meet them!

Women and children scatter chaotically among the camp. Gall and several warriors
exit.

                      GALL WIFE 1
          (to Gall Children)
          (in Sioux)
     Hokáhe íŋyaŋka po!
          (translation)
     Run, go! Hide!

                    WALTER CAMP (V.O.)
     Panic quickly turned to action as warriors left to
     gather weapons and horses to meet this new threat.

EXT. RIVER FORD A - DAY

MAIN TITLE 7A:
Ford A
12:20 P.M.

Herendeen rides up to Reno, Cooke, Keogh, and GROUP.

33

                              RENO
What is the matter now?

                           HERENDEEN
The scouts report that we've been spotted. They
killed a sentry just up a ways.

                              RENO
Very good, thank you.

Cooke is shocked by this information.

                             COOKE
                        (turns to Reno)
We'll inform the General.

Reno nods, Cooke and Keogh exit rapidly.

                              RENO
                        (to Varnum)
Charlie, get the scouts out to the front and left!

                            VARNUM
Yes sir!
                        (to the Scouts)
Let's go, there's still scouting to be done!

Varnum exits.

                     WALTER CAMP (V.O.)
And with that Reno plunged his battalion head
first towards the large Indian Camp.

                                                          CUT TO:

EXT. VALLEY FLOOR - DAY - MONTAGE

A line of one-hundred forty SOLDIERS ride across open ground.

A giant dust cloud settles over the area. The landscape bottlenecks with trees to the
left and high ground to the right.

                                                          CUT TO:

EXT. ROLLING HILLS - DAY - LATER

MAIN TITLE 8:
Benteen's Scout ends
12:30 P.M.

Gibson and six SOLDIERS sit atop a bluff overlooking a broken and desolate landscape of continuous hills and sage brush. Gibson waves to Benteen.

                    WALTER CAMP (V.O.)
          Away from the rest of the command Captain
          Benteen's frustration mounted having found no
          signs of the Indians.

Benteen gallops forward with a TRUMPETER and ORDERLY. They stop next to Gibson.

                    GIBSON
          There's no use in going any farther. There's nothin'
          out there.

Benteen surveys the land, shakes his head, then looks over to Gibson.

                    BENTEEN
               (snarky)
          Out here valley hunting! Men and horses,
          exhausted; and we've found nothin'! Gentlemen, I
          think we've done our service. We'll strike back on
          the trail as I'm sure we'll be needed elsewhere.

All exit.

INT. TENT INTERVIEW - DAY

OLD JOHN RYAN now sits in front of Walter Camp.

                    OLD JOHN RYAN
          I was the First Sergeant of Company M.

                    WALTER CAMP
          Starting with Reno's charge in the valley, he
          stopped and formed a skirmish line?

                    OLD JOHN RYAN
          Yes. We came up onto higher ground and formed a
          skirmish line from the timber towards the bluffs.

Walter Camp scribbles fanatically. Old John Ryan looks to the distance.

RENO (O.S.)
Halt! Prepare to fight on foot!

EXT. VALLEY FLOOR - DAY - CONTINUOUS

MAIN TITLE 9:
Reno's Skirmish Line
12:43 P.M.

FIRST SERGEANT JOHN RYAN; gray eyes, brown hair, fair complexion, beard; watches Reno ride up to CAPTAIN THOMAS FRENCH; hazel eyes, brown hair, fair complexion, mustache.

RENO
Captain French move your company to the left flank and keep the flankers moving forward to clear the timber. G Company will occupy the timber and secure the horses there!

French nods.

FRENCH
Yes sir!

Reno Exits. GUNSHOTS--NATIVES scurry about to the far front.

FRENCH
Sergeant Ryan, get the men deployed in skirmish order!

RYAN
Yes sir!

Ryan and SOLDIERS form a line. Horses are led in circles behind the formation. NATIVES ride to the front--WHOOPS and YELLS--lingering dust.

WALTER CAMP (V.O.)
Major Reno's thin blue line advanced slowly forward as more and more warriors came to face him.

FRENCH
Advance by fire, commence firing!

A dozen GUNSHOTS. Every other SOLDIER steps forward then stops.

Bullets HISS and POP over the riding NATIVE'S heads. They raise their rifles--BANG.

INT. TENT INTERVIEW - DAY

Walter Camp writes, stops, and looks up to Old he Dog.

> WALTER CAMP
> What can you tell me about the first attack?

> OLD HE DOG
> When Reno approached, the Hunks went out ahead, mostly on foot, to hold the soldiers back.

EXT. NATIVE VILLAGE - DAY - CONTINUOUS

He Dog watches as WARRIOR 2 runs up to Gall.

> WARRIOR 2
> (in Sioux)
> Akíčhita óta kowákataŋhaŋ yaŋkápelo čha héčhel onáwaȟ'uŋ weló.
> (translation)
> I heard there's more soldiers on the other side of river!

> GALL
> (in Sioux)
> Tokhiya hwo?
> (translation)
> Where?

> WARRIOR 2
> (in Sioux)
> Paháta anamá úŋpi na ókšaŋ anáuŋptapi.
> (translation)
> They are hiding on the hill and they are surrounding us.

Gall looks as dozens of WARRIORS ride off towards Reno.

> GALL
> (in Sioux)
> (to Warrior 2)
> Ektá wičhúŋyiŋ na waáwičauŋtuŋwaŋkiŋ ktelo. Naháŋ thiwáhe awáŋwičhauŋglakapi kta waŋ héčha!
> (translation)
> We will go there and scout them out. And we all must protect our families.

Gall and Warrior 2 ride off. He Dog exits.

WARRIORS mount horses, WHOOP, YELL, and ride off with a variety of killing devices.

> WALTER CAMP (V.O.)
> At the time of the battle, what was your rank and position?

EXT. VALLEY FLOOR - DAY - CONTINUOUS

Crazy Horse readies himself for battle.

> WALTER CAMP (V.O.)
> There are few Indian names that call forth more instant recognition and fear than that of Crazy Horse. He ranks high among the great warriors of the plains.
> (beat)
> He prepared himself for battle that day as he had done many times before.
> (dramatic pause)
> It is spoken that he knew no fear. That bullets nor arrows could ever kill him.
> (beat)
> Much of the great warrior is steeped in myth and legend; but what is not questionable, is the intensity and resolve he brought with him to any fight.

INT. TENT INTERVIEW - DAY

OLD PETER THOMPSON sits across from Walter Camp.

> WALTER CAMP
> Thompson is it?

> OLD PETER THOMPSON
> Yes sir, Peter. I was a private in Company C under Custer.

> WALTER CAMP
> How is it that you found yourself with Reno?

> OLD PETER THOMPSON
> When the companies came in sight of the village they gave the regular charging yell and urged their horses at a gallop. I was gradually left behind in spite of all I could do to keep up with my company.

EXT. ROLLING HILLS - DAY - MOMENTS LATER

SOLDIERS march on in columns.

Kanipe watches Tom Custer ride up alongside LIEUTENANT HENRY HARRINGTON.

> TOM CUSTER
> Henry, it's a large village and Reno is engaged
> below. We're pushing on North.

> HARRINGTON
> What of Benteen and the packs?

> TOM CUSTER
> They'll be along with haste. Keep the men's wits
> about them once we're in the thick of it!

> HARRINGTON
> We won't disappoint!

Tom Custer exits.

Kanipe looks around, then turns the horse and rides back the way they came.

> WALTER CAMP (V.O.)
> As the battle in the valley raged, Custer pushed his
> five companies hard to the north.

EXT. ROLLING HILLS - DAY

PRIVATE PETER THOMPSON; brown eyes, brown hair, ruddy, gruff; spurs his horse. It BLOWS and WHINNIES and moves sluggishly.

> WALTER CAMP (V.O.)
> The pace was grueling and many to the rear of the
> column found their horses giving way to
> exhaustion.

> THOMPSON
> C'mon you beast!

He spurs the horse harder--it doesn't respond. SOLDIERS pass him.

> SOLDIER 1
> What is the matter Thompson?

SOLDIERS LAUGH.

                                    THOMPSON
                        My horse is entirely played out!

SOLDIER 5 rides up to Thompson.

                                    SOLDIER 5
                        Let's keep together then?

Thompson--Disappointed expression.

                                    THOMPSON
                        Care to trade horses?

Soldier 5 gives Thompson a strange look then turns his horse to the rear and rides
away.

SERGEANT DANIEL KANIPE; hazel eyes, light hair, young; rides up.

                                    KANIPE
                        If your mount can't keep pace then take it to the
                        rear!

SOLDIERS continue passing Thompson.

                              OLD PETER THOMPSON (V.O.)
                        I figured I'd get along anyway, but my progress was
                        very slow.

INT. TENT - DAY

More words appear on the page of Walter Camp's notebook as he scribbles away.

                              WALTER CAMP (V.O.)
                        The shock of events found many of the Indian
                        women and children fleeing in all directions.

EXT. TREES - DAY

Near the water's edge in some trees, Gall Wives 1 & 2 with Gall Children 1, 2, & 3
hurry through thick foliage.

                              WALTER CAMP (V.O.)
                        Gall's family took shelter somewhere in the trees
                        to the west.

Half Yellow Face and Scouts emerge and see them. ALL stop and stare at each other.
NATIVES-fear, SCOUTS-anger.

GUNSHOTS--SCREAMS.

                                       40

EXT. ROLLING HILLS - DAY - MOMENTS LATER

MAIN TITLE 10:
The last note
1:00 P.M.

PRIVATE GIOVANI MARTINI rides along with Cooke, TRUMPETER HENRY
DOSE, SERGEANT ROBERT HUGHES, and Sharrow.

G. Custer rides up.

                         G. CUSTER
          Adjutant!

MARTINI and GROUP stop, other SOLDIERS continue to pass by.

                         COOKE
          General?

                         G. CUSTER
          Send a message to Colonel Benteen. This is a big
          village, I need him to be quick and bring the packs!

                         COOKE
          Yes sir!

                         COOKE
          Dose!

Cooke moves towards Dose then stops.

                         G. CUSTER
          Cooke, give the message to Martini. He knows
          Benteen!

                         COOKE
          Yes sir!

G. Custer exits with Hughes and GROUP.

Cooke dismounts, pulls out a notepad and pencil from a leather pouch on his saddle
and scribbles a note.

                         WALTER CAMP (V.O.)
          Perhaps one of the most ambiguous aspects of the
          battle can be found in the few simple words
          Lieutenant W.W. Cooke hastily scribbled on a
          piece of paper.
                    (dramatic pause)
          Benteen. Come on. Big village. Be quick.
                    (MORE)

41

                    WALTER CAMP (V.O.) (CONT'D)
Bring packs.
          (strong emphasis with rhythmic
           pauses)
P.S Bring packs.

He tears the page.

                    WALTER CAMP (V.O.)(CONT'D)
These were the last words that any one who
survived would hear from General Custer.

                    COOKE
          (to Martini slowly)
Martini, take this message to Colonel Benteen. Tell
him it's a big village and to bring the packs.

                    MARTINI
          (broken English)
Yes sir! I do this ting for you!

Martini grabs the note and pockets it.

                    COOKE
Tell Benteen to be quick.

                    MARTINI
Quick, yes sir!

Martini turns his horse and stops.

                    COOKE
Hurry back down our trail to Benteen. If you see
no danger then return, if you find Indians in your
way then stay with Benteen.

Martini salutes.

                    MARTINI
Yes sir!

                    COOKE
Godspeed son!

Martini exits at a gallop.

                    OLD GODFREY (V.O.)
When Benteen watered his horses at the morass he
waited some time.

INT. TENT INTERVIEW - DAY

Walter Camp looks up to Old Godfrey.

> WALTER CAMP
> After Benteen returned to the trail, he watered his horses?

> OLD GODFREY
> Some of the officers began to get uneasy, especially as we were hearing firing.

EXT. MORASS - DAY - LATER

MAIN TITLE 11:
The Morass
1:10 P.M.

> OLD GODFREY (V.O.)
> Captain Weir became especially impatient and wanted to go.

Low brush surrounds a damp mud hole. SOLDIERS some mounted and some dismounted stand along a ridge overlooking the water hole below.

Horses gulp filthy muddy water. Their mouths froth from heat exhaustion. SOLDIERS wipe their brows, several tie bandanas around their heads.

Distant GUNFIRE--SOLDIERS look.

CAPTAIN THOMAS WEIR; gray eyes, brown hair, light complexion, mustache; looks and pauses as the sounds continue. He can see nothing but broken terrain. He urges his horse forward.

Godfrey watches as Weir rides up and stops.

> GODFREY
> Captain Weir?

> WEIR
> I wonder why the old man is keeping us here so long.

> GODFREY
> I suppose he's giving the men a chance to fill their canteens.

Weir shakes his head and rides up to Benteen.

43

                              WEIR
          Hadn't we better go to the sound of the firing?

                              BENTEEN
          Captain Weir, the horses are exhausted and haven't
          had water since last night. Go with your company!

                              WEIR
          We ought to be over there!

Weir points towards the SOUNDS of battle.

                              BENTEEN
          We'll be on it presently, now return to your
          company!

Weir SCOFFS, SPITS, and exits.

INT. TENT INTERVIEW - DAY

Old Godfrey looks as Walter Camp writes furiously.

                              OLD GODFREY
          I thought all was over and we'd have nothing to
          do except go up and congratulate the others.

EXT. MORASS - DAY - MOMENTS LATER

Godfrey rides up to Benteen.

                              GODFREY
          Captain Weir is an impatient one.

                              BENTEEN
          I suppose he's anxious to go and find his General.

Godfrey smiles--CHUCKLES.

                              BENTEEN (CONT'D)
          We'll be along shortly, ready your company behind
          Weir.

                              GODFREY
          Yes sir!

Godfrey exits. Benteen stares into the distance.

<u>INT. TENT INTERVIEW - DAY</u>

Walter Camp looks up from his writing to Old Foolish Elk.

                    WALTER CAMP
          What do you recollect of the first bit of fighting?

                    OLD FOOLISH ELK
          It started at the Hunkpapa teepees. Men from all
          tribes who had their horses grabbed their guns and
          went up the river to join in the fight.

<u>EXT. VALLEY FLOOR - DAY</u>

<u>MAIN TITLE 12:</u>
<u>Reno's Skirmish Line</u>
<u>1:10 P.M.</u>

A dust cloud thickens around French and his SOLDIERS. They move forward, stop,
BANG--forward, stop, BANG. He Dog SHOOTS.

                    WALTER CAMP (V.O.)
          Major Reno watched with trepidation as hordes of
          warriors slowly began engulfing his companies.

NATIVE WARRIORS ride amongst the dust--NATIVE WHOOPS crescendo.

A WARRIOR emerges from the dust--BANG-he falls dead.

                    OLD HE DOG (V.O.)
          We were getting ready for word to charge in a
          body on the soldiers at the timber. The Sioux had
          not all got there yet, but Indians from all tribes--all
          that could get horses were there.

Reno watches the line. CAPTAIN MYLES MOYLAN rides up.

                    MOYLAN
          Sir, the Indians are getting into our flanks!

Reno looks in several directions taking everything in.

                    RENO
          Where the hell is Custer?
                    (beat)
          Order your company to pull back to the brow of
          the timber! We'll use the trees for cover!

Moylan nods and gallops off.

WALTER CAMP (V.O.)
The pressure on Reno to act mounted.

INT. TENT INTERVIEW - DAY

John Ryan looks distant then over to Walter Camp.

WALTER CAMP
The Indians came to meet you in force?

OLD JOHN RYAN
We fired volleys into the Indians, repulsing their charges.

WALTER CAMP
The Indians, they turned your skirmish line?

OLD JOHN RYAN
Correct. They couldn't cut through us, so they commenced to circle. They eventually closed in on the rear.

EXT. VALLEY FLOOR - DAY

Ryan watches SOLDIERS SHOOT.

RYAN
Alright boys we're going to fall back to the horses. Retire by fire, commence firing!

Every other SOLDIER fires then moves to the rear and stops.

OLD JOHN RYAN (V.O.)
We had orders to fall back to our horses. This is where the first man was killed, Sergeant Miles O'hara.

Morris SHOOTS his rifle and follows several SOLDIERS to the rear.

He looks and sees SERGEANT MILES O'HARA; gray eyes, light hair, ruddy complexion; kneeling. He SHOOTS at NATIVES to his left.

MORRIS
Come on, O'Hara! We are falling back to our horses!

O'Hara doesn't hear Morris. BANG--SQUISH--BLOOD. A bullet hits O'Hara in the chest. He staggers and falls to the ground. Morris and Ryan watch.

46

MORRIS

O'Hara!

He moves to run, Ryan grabs him.

RYAN

He's gone, now fall back to the horses!

Ryan throws Morris towards the horses. Morris stumbles, looks, and runs to the horses.

O'Hara lays on his back. He looks towards the SOLDIERS leaving.

O'HARA
(gasping for air)
For God's sake, don't leave me.
(gasps more)
Don't leave me.

His eyes glaze over--dead. Ryan stops and stares momentarily towards O'Hara.

INT. TENT INTERVIEW - DAY

Old combat AMBIENCE fades.

Old John Ryan pauses then breathes.

OLD JOHN RYAN
O'Hara had only been promoted to Sergeant days
before. He was a fine soldier and we missed him
very much.

Walter Camp pauses to let the tension of the moment play out, he looks to his notebook then up.

WALTER CAMP
The Indians then encircled the trees where you
were?

Old John Ryan looks to Walter Camp.

OLD JOHN RYAN
They strung us out and began to circle, yes. We
moved to some trees when we saw Moylan's
company doing so.

EXT. RENO TIMBER DEFENSE - DAY - CONTINUOUS

SOLDIERS take cover behind a bank with heavy shrubbery and trees covering them.

MAIN TITLE 13:
Reno Moves Into The Timber
1:20 P.M.

Horses WHINNY and buck around--bullets CRACK through the trees. Soldiers SHOOT.

Reno looks left and ride. French and Moylan approach and stop.

                    FRENCH
        We're gonna need the packs, soon!

                    MOYLAN
        The boys are doing good; but we're gonna need
        more ammo!

WARRIORS SHOOT along the wood line towards SOLDIERS while other WARRIORS ride around.

                    WALTER CAMP (V.O.)
        Major Reno found himself surrounded under ever
        increasing fire from three sides.

                    RENO
              (to the group)
        We were promised support, but if we run out of
        ammo we're through! The entire Sioux nation is
        right out of those trees!
              (beat)
        Gentlemen, this position is quickly becoming
        untenable!

                    FRENCH
        I concur.

Bullets SNAP overhead, a tree branch falls, ALL duck slightly.

                    RENO
        Prepare your companies to leave. We're
        surrounded and the only way out of here is back
        the way we came.

BANG--BANG--BANG--bullets CRASH through the trees. SCREAMS of pain echo.

EXT. VALLEY FLOOR - DAY - CONTINUOUS

Crazy Horse rides along the trees with He Dog, Foolish Elk, Standing Black Bear, and WARRIORS. They SHOOT into the trees--SOLDIERS SHOOT back.

> WALTER CAMP (V.O.)
> How would you describe this fight in the timber?

Horse HOOVES beat hard, Native war WHOOPS--BANG, BANG, BANG--smoke and dust rise high over the valley floor.

> OLD JOHN RYAN (V.O.)
> The Indians fired into us on all sides, they had us surrounded.

EXT. RENO TIMBER DEFENSE - DAY - CONTINUOUS

> OLD JOHN RYAN (V.O.)
> Private George Lorentz was shot and dropped to the ground.

Ryan watches a bullet hit a SOLDIER in the head who collapses.

Reno and Bloody Knife wrangle their horses.

> RENO
> Bloody Knife! What are the Indians doing?

BANG--BANG--BANG. A bullet hits Bloody Knife in the face--blood sprays, Reno watches the lifeless body fall hard to the ground.

> RENO
> Jesus!
>   (screaming)
> Mount!

SOLDIERS mount their horses. BANG-SOLDIER 7 falls grabbing a bloody wound near Reno.

> SOLDIER 7
> Oh my god! I've had it!

Soldier 7 SCREAMS in pain. Reno snaps a look then over to French who is organizing SOLDIERS on their horses.

> RENO
> Captain French, we're charging out of here! Mount your damn horse!

Reno rides away.

> WALTER CAMP (V.O.)
> Thus began Reno's movement out of the timber and into the annuals of scrutiny.
>   (MORE)

WALTER CAMP (V.O.) (CONT'D)

Some called it a charge, others a retreat; but it was
a decision that would haunt him for the rest of his
life.

FRENCH (O.S.)

John mount the men and get a move on!

RYAN

Yes sir!

OLD JOHN RYAN (V.O.)

The order was given to charge, and away we went.

French and SOLDIERS exit rapidly.

INT. TENT INTERVIEW - DAY

Old Foolish Elk stares into the distance.

WALTER CAMP

How long did the fighting take place?

Old Foolish Elk looks to Walter Camp.

OLD FOOLISH ELK

The fight didn't last long and before the larger part
of Indians could get there, we had chased the
soldiers out of the river valley and up into the
bluffs.

WALTER CAMP

What route did they take?

OLD FOOLISH ELK

We forced the soldiers across the river at the
nearest point they could.

EXT. VALLEY FLOOR - DAY - MOMENTS LATER

OLD FOOLISH ELK (V.O.)

They couldn't go back from where they had come
from.

SOLDIERS emerge from the trees at a full gallop.

50

<u>EXT. VALLEY FLOOR - DAY - MOMENTS LATER</u>

> OLD JOHN RYAN (V.O.)
> The fighting was hand to hand, and it was death to
> any man who couldn't keep up.

Charley Reynolds's races out of the trees into an opening. He aims his rifle--BANG.

> CHARLEY REYNOLDS
> You're gonna pay for it dearly!

He aims--Bang. He moves to load, a WARRIOR runs up and beats Charley Reynolds
viciously with a club.

<u>INT. TENT INTERVIEW - DAY</u>

Old Varnum's face is one of sadness.

> OLD VARNUM
> I didn't hear any orders, but everyone was
> mounted. Men were calling that they were going to
> make a charge, so I mounted my horse.

> WALTER CAMP
> What can you recall on retreating from the timber?

> OLD VARNUM
> I left the timber late, but I had a fast horse so I
> overtook the head of the column quickly.

> WALTER CAMP
> Would you say it was a necessary movement?

> OLD VARNUM
> We were not only surrounded, but the odds against
> us were so fearful that we were obliged to retreat.

> WALTER CAMP
> But you heard it was a charge?

Old Varnum looks distant.

<u>EXT. RIVER RETREAT CROSSING - DAY - CONTINUOUS</u>

> OLD VARNUM (V.O.)
> I suppose there had been a charge started, and the
> first few out came across some Indians and were
> turned towards the river.

51

MAIN TITLE 14:
Reno's retreat
1:30 P.M.

Horses plunge into the river as SOLDIERS spur them harder. SOLDIERS on foot race the edge of the river and run in.

Varnum reaches the river bank. Soldiers flee frantically across the river on horse a SOLDIER is hit and falls into the water.

> VARNUM
> Stop! Stop!

No one pays any attention. He spurs his horse across and rides up the bank and immediately up a small crevice to a ridge.

> RYAN
> Lieutenant, c'mon! Back to the command! This
> way!

Varnum turns his horse and gallops away.

> WALTER CAMP (V.O.)
> The gauntlet of death that Reno's soldiers endured
> resulted in thirty-three of his men killed.

INT. TENT INTERVIEW - DAY

He Dog looks over to Walter Camp.

> WALTER CAMP
> Is this when Custer was seen?

> OLD HE DOG
> We looked and saw other soldiers coming on the
> big hill over east.

> WALTER CAMP
> And what were they doing?

> OLD HE DOG
> When Custer passed near to Ford B, he was
> moving as though to reach the lower end of our
> camp.

<u>EXT. MEDICINE TAIL COULEE - DAY - CONTINUOUS</u>

Gall approaches some brush, stops, and looks--two-hundred ten SOLDIERS amass in Medicine Tail Coulee.

                    OLD HE DOG (V.O.)
          They kept right on down the river and crossed
          Medicine Tail coulee and onto a little rise.

<u>MAIN TITLE 15:</u>
<u>Medicine Tail Coulee</u>
<u>1:30 P.M.</u>

G. Custer scans the horizon with his binoculars and sees distant teepees. He drops the binoculars and looks to Yates.

                    G. CUSTER
          Benteen ought to be along so there's no time to
          delay. Colonel Yates, you will proceed with your
          battalion forward towards the Ford. I want to get
          a good look of the area and see what the Indians
          are doing.

                    YATES
          Yes sir!

                    G. CUSTER
          We have to be quick. I want to be able to pitch
          into the camp as soon as Colonel Benteen arrives.

Yates exits. G. Custer turns to Keogh.

                    G. CUSTER
          Colonel Keogh, you'll take your companies to the
          high ground to our flank there.

                    KEOGH
          Very well General.

G. Custer exits, Keogh exits.

LIEUTENANT ALGERNON SMITH; brown eyes, brown hair, mustache; watches Yates approach.

                    YATES
          Lieutenant Smith, we'll move towards the Ford.
               (points)
                         (MORE)

53

> YATES (CONT'D)
> I want Company E to screen our front and left, F
> will go to the high ground with General Custer!

> ALGERNON SMITH
> Understood!

BOTH exit.

> OLD GODFREY (V.O.)
> I don't know where Trumpeter Martin came up
> with the message, but it was a good distance from
> where we watered the horses.

EXT. ROLLING HILLS - DAY - CONTINUOUS

Benteen watches Martini ride at a gallop. He raises his hand, SOLDIERS stop in a
column behind.

> BENTEEN
> Battalion, halt!

> OFFICER (O.S.)
> Company halt.

Benteen with Weir, Gibson, and Edgerly ride forward. Martini rides up and stops. He
salutes Benteen and hands him a folded piece of paper. Benteen reads it silently,
PUFFS, then hands it to Weir.

> BENTEEN
> (to Martini)
> Where's the General now?

> MARTINI
> A few miles up. It's a big village.

> BENTEEN
> And where are the hostiles?

Martini-confused.

> BENTEEN
> (frustrated)
> The Indians? The big village, where is it?

> MARTINI
> The Indians, they skedaddling.

Benteen SCOFFS, Weir hands the note back to Benteen who sticks it into his pocket.

                              BENTEEN
              You will ride with H Company.

                              MARTINI
              Yes sir!

Martini exits.

                              BENTEEN
                         (to Edgerly and Weir)
              The packs are safe to our rear, I don't see a need to
              go back for them.

Distant sporadic GUNSHOTS. ALL look.

                         BENTEEN (CONTD)
              I also don't think that we sit here and wait.

Weir immediately turns his horse and rides back to his company.

                              WEIR
              At the trot, forward, march!

Benteen shakes his head and turns to Gibson.

                              BENTEEN
                         (escalating anger)
              I was supposed to have the advance and now I am
              following up the packs!

Gibson nods, All exit rapidly.

INT. TENT INTERVIEW - DAY

Walter Camp looks up to Old Foolish Elk.

                         WALTER CAMP
              Was there any fighting with Custer at the river
              crossing?

                         OLD FOOLISH ELK
              The soldiers fired across the river into the village
              without getting into it.

                         WALTER CAMP
              Were any of Custer's soldiers killed there?

OLD FOOLISH ELK
I heard that one man rode his horse into the village
and was killed.

EXT. RIVER FORD B - DAY - CONTINUOUS

MAIN TITLE 16:
Near Ford B
2:00 P.M.

Algernon Smith turns to LIEUTENANT JAMES STURGIS; dark eyes, dark hair, fair
complexion, looks young; looks along the horizon.

OLD HE DOG (V.O.)
There a few shots down there--no general fighting.
Fifteen or twenty Sioux on east side of river, but
not much shooting.

A WARRIOR with a HENRY RIFLE creeps into some brush and takes aim.

ALGERNON SMITH
Sturgis, take your platoon and deploy on the left
flank.

STURGIS
Yes sir.

BANG--a bullet hits Sturgis, he slumps in the saddle, his horse races off. Algernon
Smith looks on in contempt.

WALTER CAMP (V.O.)
General Custer's exact movements cannot be
known, but evidence suggests that he split his
forces somewhere along the march to the river and
he began skirmishing as he continued to the north.

Gall runs up behind cover to a clearing near the river. He and several WARRIORS
grab rifles and take cover in some brush.

OLD HE DOG (V.O.)
Before the big fight started, we drove Custer up a
ridge. Then he went down along a hollow and
passed the soldiers.

SOLDIERS SHOOT. Bullets HISS and POP overhead. SOLDIERS SHOOT then
fall back towards their horses.

<u>INT. TENT INTERVIEW - DAY</u>

Walter Camp scribbles and doesn't look up.

> WALTER CAMP
> And this is when Captain Benteen met Major Reno
> on the hills?

> OLD GODFREY
> We came on Colonel Reno with his companies. I
> learned they had charged over the plain and had a
> big fight in the woods.

> WALTER CAMP
> What was the state of the men?

<u>EXT. RENO HILL - DAY - MOMENTS LATER</u>

> OLD GODFREY (V.O.)
> They were whipped and were damn glad to see us.

Weary eyed SOLDIERS hunker about a wide hilly area.

<u>MAIN TITLE 17:</u>
<u>Benteen arrives on Reno Hill</u>
<u>2:00 P.M.</u>

Reno hopelessly fires his pistol towards a small group of WARRIORS that are too far
away to hit.

Benteen races to Reno.

> BENTEEN
> Major Reno?

> RENO
> For God's sake, Benteen, halt your command and
> help me. I've lost half my men!

> BENTEEN
> Where's Custer?

> RENO
> I have no idea where Custer is. I was ordered to
> attack with the promise that he'd support me...I
> haven't seen him since!

INT. TENT - DAY

The words "where was Custer" are shown on Walter Camp's notebook.

> WALTER CAMP (V.O.)
> Where was Custer?

Walter Camp continues writing.

> WALTER CAMP (V.O.) (CONT'D)
> That seems to be a question paramount to all and asked frequently.

EXT. RENO HILL - DAY - MOMENTS LATER

Benteen pulls out the message he received and hands it to Reno.

> BENTEEN
> I wonder if this is to be another Major Elliot affair?

Reno stares momentarily at Benteen then reads the message.

> BENTEEN
> I think it is Custer who has forgotten us!

Reno looks up without disagreement and hands the note back to Benteen.

> RENO
> We have wounded and are desperately short on ammo.

> BENTEEN (CONTD)
> I'll organize my companies in skirmish order and have the men spare some rounds!

Reno nods, Benteen exits.

INT. TENT INTERVIEW - DAY

Old Foolish Elk waits for Walter Camp to stop writing.

> WALTER CAMP
> Where did Custer go after leaving Medicine Tail Coulee?

> OLD FOOLISH ELK
> The soldiers went to the high ground near where they made their first stand.

Old Foolish Elk points to the area of Calhoun Hill on the map.

                    WALTER CAMP
          Was this around the place known as Calhoun Hill?

                    OLD FOOLISH ELK
          Yes. Many soldiers stayed, but Custer and other
          soldiers went on to other end of the camp.

Old Foolish Elk points at the area of Ford D.

EXT. CALHOUN HILL - DAY

MAIN TITLE 18:
Calhoun Hill
2:45 P.M.

Dozens of SOLDIERS fire down from the top of Calhoun Hill as WARRIORS
swarm about int he distance. GUNFIRE and bullet POPS echo.

                    WALTER CAMP (V.O.)
          Leaving three companies to defend Calhoun Hill,
          Custer took two companies and marched further
          north to find a river crossing.

Keogh approaches Calhoun.

                    KEOGH
          Calhoun, there's Indians in our rear. I'm going to
          take I Company and block them. Keep the line in
          order!

                    CALHOUN
          Yes sir!

Keogh exits.

                    OLD FOOLISH ELK (V.O.)
          We were between Custer and the river and all the
          time coming up and getting around him.

WARRIORS SHOOT, distant SOLDIERS on Calhoun Hill SHOOT back. Other
WARRIORS crawl through ravines and coulees with bows and arrows to close with
the hill.

                    GALL
               (in Sioux)
          Khúta po! Khúta po! Uŋmápi kiŋ lená úpelo.
               (MORE)

                    GALL (CONT'D)
                        (translation)
            Keep shooting! Other Warriors are coming!

They stop and fling arrows into the air.

Arrows hit near SOLDIERS on the hill. Gall watches.

BANG--BANG--BANG.

                    OLD FOOLISH ELK (V.O.)
            The soldiers charged twice but could not drive us
            away, then the battle became furious.

EXT. GREASY GRASS RIDGE - DAY - MOMENTS LATER

Distant trumpet SOUNDS "Charge." Horses charge in and stop. SOLDIERS
SHOOT at WARRIORS

                    WALTER CAMP (V.O.)
            In a particularly ambitious move, Company C led
            by Lieutenant Harrington charged off Calhoun Hill
            to attack warriors threatening the hill.

LAME WHITE MAN; dark eyes, dark hair, Native American; jumps up amidst the
warriors.

                    LAME WHITE MAN
                        (in Sioux)
            Íŋyáŋka šni yo. Kakhíya húŋ□ lala yankápi. Kú wo!
                        (translation)
            Don't run! There is only a few soldiers. Come back!
                        (waves arm)
                        (in Sioux)

            Ú po! Iyúha wičháuŋktepi uŋkókihipi kteló.
            Mihákab u po!
                        (translation)
            Come, we can kill them all! Follow me!

ALL run at the soldiers, Native WHOOPS echo loudly.

Harrington watches the WARRIORS approach.

                    HARRINGTON
            Dismount! Fight on foot!

SOLDIERS scramble from their horses.

HARRINGTON

Form a skirmish line, forward!

Lame White Man and WARRIORS charge up and club several SOLDIERS. The soldiers break and move in separate directions.

Harrington watches as SOLDIERS flee aimlessly.

HARRINGTON

Hold your ground! Hold it men!

A WARRIOR approaches, Harrington SHOOTS him. Another WARRIOR, Harrington SHOOTS, the WARRIOR falls dead. Harrington turns his horse and SHOOTS another WARRIOR.

HARRINGTON

Retreat--retreat!

BANG--Harrington slumps in his saddle. The horse takes off.

WALTER CAMP (V.O.)

Harrington's move quickly turned into a route as dozens of warriors led by Cheyenne Chief Lame White Man charged the small force from all directions.

SOLDIERS flee along the ridge. WARRIORS bash, hack, and slash other SOLDIERS until there are none left.

EXT. CALHOUN HILL - DAY - CONTINUOUS

MAIN TITLE 19:
Calhoun Hill
3:00 P.M.

Calhoun turns to LIEUTENANT JOHN CRITTENDEN; dark eyes, dark hair, beard, glass eye.

CALHOUN

Lieutenant Crittenden!

Crittenden looks, Calhoun points towards the ridge.

CALHOUN (CONT'D)

Move your platoon to the west and cover Harrington! He's in a bad spot!

61

                    CRITTENDEN
Understood!
          (to his soldiers)
Listen up, we're repositioning to the cusp of the
ridge there!
          (points)
Pick your shots carefully, C Company is getting
beat up down there! As skirmishers, march!

Crittenden and SOLDIERS stop along the cusp of the hill.

                    CRITTENDEN
Halt! Four hundred yards, commence firing!

Dozens of GUNSHOTS.

Gall watches as SOLDIERS shift around on the hill. They look over and see Lame
White Man and WARRIORS fighting hard with other SOLDIERS.

                      GALL
          (in Sioux)
Natáŋ po! Mihákab po!
          (translation)
Attack! Follow me!

Gall and WARRIORS charge towards the hill.

                    WALTER CAMP (V.O.)
Mounting pressure on Calhoun Hill forced the
soldiers of Company L back as Chief Gall led
hordes of warriors over the cusp of the hill.

SOLDIERS SHOOT frantically at the WARRIORS who duck and cover behind
brush, SHOOT, then come closer.

Calhoun watches as the WARRIORS come close to his line.

                    CALHOUN
Retire by fire! Retire by fire!

Crittenden looks back then to his SOLDIERS.

                    CRITTENDEN
Fall back! Back, to the horses!

SOLDIERS SHOOT then move back then SHOOT again.

Calhoun watches as WARRIORS crest the top of Calhoun Hill.

62

CALHOUN

Dear God!

Crittenden looks to Calhoun. BANG--a bullet hits Calhoun, he falls dead. Crittenden runs over to Calhoun and checks him. He SHOOTS. SOLDIERS run by in full flight.

CRITTENDEN
Cowards! Cover the withdrawal!

WALTER CAMP (V.O.)
In an attempt to cover the withdrawal,
Lieutenants Calhoun and Crittenden were killed,
falling only feet from one another.

BANG--Crittenden falls dead next to Calhoun.

OLD HE DOG (V.O.)
The Keogh soldiers had gone down to a low spot
behind the hill. This is where Crazy Horse charged.

EXT. SWALE - DAY

Crazy Horse, He Dog, Foolish Elk, Standing Black Bear, and WARRIORS crest the top of a ridge. Keogh looks, Crazy Horse looks.

WALTER CAMP (V.O.)
In a place known as the Swale, Captain Keogh
found himself impaled on the horns of a dilemma.

Keogh lays clutching a bloody leg wound. He sees Crazy Horse on the ridge.

KEOGH
To the west! Commence firing!

SOLDIERS quickly load their rifles and SHOOT at Crazy Horse. ALL quickly retreat back behind the ridge.

CRAZY HORSE
(in Sioux)
Húŋȟlala na iyúha wakȟókpȟapi. Blihíč'iya po!
(translation)
There are only a few of them and they are scared.
Have courage!

Crazy Horse charges alone over the ridge. SOLDIERS SHOOT, as Crazy Horse rides by WHOOPING and YELLS--WARRIORS watch.

HE DOG
     (in Sioux)
Hókahé ikíčhize wičáša ! Lé aŋpétu kiŋ t'á
wastékeló!
     (translation)
Come on Warriors! It is a good day to die!

ALL charge into the SOLDIERS.

OLD HE DOG (V.O.)
We broke through and split up soldiers in two
bunches.

SOLDIERS and WARRIORS mix together in hand to hand combat. SOLDIERS die
in various horrendous forms--WARRIORS fall dead--blood splatters through the air.

OLD HE DOG (V.O.)
We killed all the soldiers there.

Crazy Horse, He Dog, and Foolish Elk along the soldiers shooting into them.

White Man crosses the front--BANG--he falls dead.

WALTER CAMP (V.O.)
Mortally wounded, Keogh could only lay there...
     (beat)
Delaying the inevitable.

OLD HE DOG (V.O.)
We killed all the soldiers there.

Crazy Horse, He Dog, and Foolish Elk along the soldiers shooting into them.

WALTER CAMP (V.O.)
The hand to hand fighting became so brutal that
the ground ran red with blood.

Lame White Man crosses the front--BANG--he falls dead.

WALTER CAMP (V.O.)
A nightmarish hell that few can fathom.
     (dramatic pause)
And then it was over.

Keogh looks left--SOLDIERS run and die. A WARRIOR races into the violence and
brings a club down on Keogh's face.

<u>EXT. WEIR POINT - DAY</u>

                        OLD GODFREY (V.O.)
Weir went to get permission but changed his mind,
and went to scout the bluffs first. Edgerly saw
Weir heading off and supposed it was alright and
started off after him.

Weir and Sergeant 2 stand atop the apex of several peaks looking ahead at a
whirlwind cloud of dust and smoke. Distant GUNFIRE and Native WHOOPS echo
around the hills.

MAIN TITLE 20:
<u>Weir Point</u>
<u>3:10 P.M.</u>

                        WALTER CAMP (V.O.)
On a high ridge known Captain Weir tried to
ascertain the whereabouts of General Custer...

Weir looks through binoculars.

                        WEIR
I can't see a damned thing!

                        SERGEANT 2
Here sir, try my looking glasses.

Weir and Sergeant 2 trade binoculars. Weir looks again.

                        WEIR
I still can't make out anything. There's just too far
away!

Edgerly walks to the top next to Weir.

                        WALTER CAMP (V.O.)
But three miles through smoke and dust made the
endeavor fruitless.

                        EDGERLY
Anything of Custer?

                        WEIR
It's quite some distance, but he is somewhere
there, beyond the horizon slightly--amongst all that
smoke and dust!

Weir hands the binoculars to Edgerly who puts them to his face. He scans the horizon--some distant figures riding around shooting at the ground. He hands the binoculars back to Weir.

                    EDGERLY
          Can't make out much. It looks as though the
          Indians are just riding around shooting the ground.

FOOTSTEPS to the rear--ALL look. Benteen quickly climbs to the summit next to Weir with SWALLOW TAIL GUIDON in hand. Benteen looks and for the first time sees the vast size of the Native village.

                    BENTEEN
          My God--This is a hell of a place to fight Indians.

                    WEIR
          Best I can tell is General Custer is over those ridges
          somewhere.

Benteen jams his company guidon into the ground.

INT. TENT INTERVIEW - DAY

Walter Camp writes then looks up to Old Foolish Elk.

                    WALTER CAMP
          Did Custer stay on the hill once he got there?

                    OLD FOOLISH ELK
          Soldiers on foot were shooting as they passed
          along. When the horses got to the top of the ridge
          the horses became mixed and soldiers were in
          confusion.

EXT. WEIR POINT - DAY

Reno reaches the top of the point with Weir and Benteen. He surveys the village and the massive dust cloud to the north.

                    RENO
          There must be a thousand lodges along this
          damned river! Where is Custer?

                    BENTEEN
          I can't tell. It seems he's retreating to the north.

WEIR

Perhaps he's headed to get relief from General
Terry?

BENTEEN

Maybe.
(pause)
This position isn't tenable. Eventually the Indians
are gonna come for us.

RENO

We'll withdraw back to our previous position.
Pass word to the companies that we're gonna fall
back to our original position on the hill.

BENTEEN

Yes sir!

ALL exit. Reno stares into the distance pondering where G. Custer might be.

WALTER CAMP (V.O.)

History has been harsh to Major Reno following
the battle.
(beat)
His detractors say he was a coward, a drunk, and
derelict in his duties
(beat)
Others say it was simply too desperate a situation
and General Custer paid the price for going a ridge
too far.

INT. TENT INTERVIEW - DAY

Old Godfrey sits waiting for Walter Camp to catch up on his writing.

OLD GODFREY

We heard volley firing and the rattle of the guns,
but no tidings of General Custer.

WALTER CAMP

Were there any thoughts on where Custer may be?

OLD GODFREY

No. We thought it strange that he did not make his
way back to us.

EXT. LAST STAND HILL - DAY - MOMENTS LATER

MAIN TITLE 21:
Last Stand Hill
3:45 P.M.

A bugler SOUNDS "Rally."

> WALTER CAMP (V.O.)
> General Custer returned from his excursion to the
> north to find his companies in ruin.

G. Custer rises from behind a dead horse and aims his rifle--BANG.

> WALTER CAMP (V.O.)
> Unable to reunite his command, he took haven on
> the highest ground he could find.
> (beat)
> A place we today call Last Stand Hill.

Arrows hit around the hill, bullets kick up dust next to SOLDIERS.

> YATES
> Keep firing! Shoot the horses for cover!

> SOLDIER 1
> (turns to his left and right)
> I need more ammo!

SOLDIERS shoot, two SOLDIERS run to cover. GUNSHOTS - left and right.

> WALTER CAMP (V.O.)
> The Indians peppered the hill with arrows and rifle
> fire from all sides, but the defense was stiff and
> determined.

A shell casing falls to the earth and bounces before coming to a stop next to other shell casings

INT. TENT INTERVIEW - DAY

> WALTER CAMP
> Did Custer stay on the hill once he got there?

> OLD FOOLISH ELK
> Soldiers on foot were shooting as they passed
> along. The Indians were so numerous that the
> soldiers could go no further, and they knew they
> were going to die.

EXT. LAST STAND HILL - DAY - CONTINUOUS

A bullet hits Yates, he falls dead. Tom Custer watches as an arrow hits Cooke in the back, he falls.

TOM CUSTER

Cooke!

WALTER CAMP (V.O.)

One by one, the soldiers around Custer fell dead or wounded.
        (beat)
His men, his officers, his friends, his family...
        (dramatic pause)
Even General Custer was finally felled by an Indian's bullet.

Tom Custer and Soldier 1 run over to Cooke and drag him back. Tom Custer looks, Foolish Elk, He Dog, Standing Black Bear and WARRIORS creep up from behind.

TOM CUSTER

To the rear!

He aims his rifle and SHOOTS.G. Custer aims his rifle--a bullet hits him in the chest, he SCREAMS--Tom Custer Looks. G. Custer slumps behind a dead horse and cups the bloody wound with his left hand.

WALTER CAMP (V.O.)

Warriors such as Crazy Horse, Gall, He Dog, and Foolish Elk continued to tighten the noose around the defender's necks.

WARRIORS crest the hill behind Tom Custer. G. Custer unholsters a pistol with his right hand and SHOOTS--a WARRIOR falls dead.

WALTER CAMP (V.O.)

Eventually came the final rush and the coup de grace was landed to those few left.

Tom Custer wheels around and swings his rifle as a club knocking a WARRIOR down. Another WARRIOR runs in and clubs Tom Custer, he falls blood pouring from his head.

WALTER CAMP (V.O.)

What anguished thoughts must have gone through the General's mind in those final fleeting moments as he lay with a gapping wound in his chest?

G. Custer raises his pistol with evident strain and SHOOTS then his arm drops--raspy BREATHING, HEARTBEAT slows. He watches--A WARRIOR bashes Tom Custer's head repeatedly.

> WALTER CAMP (V.O.)
> Did the boy General resist to his dying breath or did he succumb to his wounds before the epic conclusion?

G. Custer's eyes, frothy BREATHING. An out of focus WARRIOR points his pistol and SHOOTS.

HEARTBEAT stops.

WARRIORS hack and slash SOLDIERS.

INT. TENT INTERVIEW - DAY

Old Godfrey rubs his hands together--anxiety.

> WALTER CAMP
> Are you, or were you made aware of what was seen of General Custer's forces?

> OLD GODFREY
> We got on some very high bluffs and large numbers of Indians were seen about two miles away.
> (beat)
> But the firing had ceased except for the occasional shot.

> WALTER CAMP
> Did the Indians pursue Reno?

> OLD GODFREY
> On spotting us on the hill, the Indians directed all their attention towards us.

> WALTER CAMP
> What were your actions?

> OLD GODFREY
> I formed a skirmish line while the rest retreated. We gave the Indians a reception with such warmth that they did not attempt to come nearer than the ridge in any number.

> WALTER CAMP
> Were any men killed or wounded in this maneuver?

OLD GODFREY

There were two or three wounded in the other companies and one poor fella killed who fell in the hands of the enemy.

WALTER CAMP

Was that Private Vincent Charley?

OLD GODFREY

Yes.

EXT. LAST STAND HILL - DAY - MOMENTS LATER

WARRIORS pick over items from DEAD SOLDIERS. WOUNDED SOLDIER 6 crawls while two WARRIORS follow him. He stops and flips on his back.

WOUNDED SOLDIER 6

Please God, spare me!

He tries to crawl further. BANG. Blood erupts from his head.

WALTER CAMP (V.O.)

The reality of it all is far more grim than words can describe the sickening ghastly horror of what followed.

A WARRIOR crouches over Wounded Soldier 6 and scalps him.

INT. TENT INTERVIEW - DAY

Battle SOUNDS fade away, Old Foolish Elk stares vacant towards the horizon.

WALTER CAMP

What can you tell me of when the fighting ended?

Old Foolish Elks hesitates then looks to Walter Camp.

OLD FOOLISH ELK

After killing all the Custer soldiers, some went to attack the other soldiers on the hill.

WALTER CAMP

Were the dead soldiers scalped?

OLD FOOLISH ELK

We captured many horses that weren't wounded.
Squaws followed the course of the battle and
stripped the dead.

WALTER CAMP

Were any of the soldiers only wounded?

OLD FOOLISH ELK

I don't know. I did not stay to see any of the
wounded soldiers killed. Most of them must have
been killed during the battle.

EXT. RENO HILL - DAY - LATER

OLD GODFREY (V.O.)

Horses and packs were put in a swale and we
formed skirmishes around it. The packs were
unloaded and used for breastworks.

SOLDIERS carry WOUNDED SOLDIERS to a low area where Doctor Porter tends
to other WOUNDED SOLDIERS. His bloody hands work feverishly applying a
bandage to a badly WOUNDED SOLDIER.

MAIN TITLE 22:
Reno's defense begins
4:30 P.M.

Godfrey looks from Benteen to his SOLDIERS.

GODFREY

Dig in men! Use whatever ya got!

WALTER CAMP (V.O.)

Major Reno's command formed a circular
perimeter around the high ground, and dug in for
hard fight.

Men take out knives and other simple tools and scratch at the earth, even with their
bare hands.

SOLDIERS scurry and grab boxes and toss them near DOCTOR HENRY PORTER.

OLD JOHN RYAN (V.O.)

We dismounted with haste, putting the wounded
in a low depression on the bluffs. Doc Porter went
to work best he could patchin' men up.

72

SOLDIERS carry WOUNDED SOLDIERS to a low area where Doctor Porter tends to other WOUNDED SOLDIERS. His bloody hands work feverishly applying a bandage to a badly WOUNDED SOLDIER.

> WALTER CAMP (V.O.)
> The fighting kept up?

INT. TENT INTERVIEW - DAY

Old John Ryan looks up.

> OLD JOHN RYAN
> Very much so. One Indian in particular, I must give credit for being a good shot.

> WALTER CAMP
> Can you elaborate?

> OLD JOHN RYAN
> There was a high ridge on the right of our line.

EXT. RENO HILL - DAY - CONTINUOUS

> OLD JOHN RYAN (V.O.)
> While lying in our line he fired a shot and killed the fourth man on my right.

MAIN TITLE 23:
Reno Hill
5:15 P.M.

Bullet HISS, blood splatters, distant GUNSHOT--Ryan and French look. A SOLDIER collapses dead on the line.

> FRENCH
> Christ!

Ryan looks over.

> RYAN
> Captain French, you should take cover sir!

French takes cover with Ryan.

Bullet HISS, blood splatters, distant GUNSHOT--another SOLDIER collapses dead.

> FRENCH
> Where in the hell is that coming from Sergeant?

                              RYAN
              Must be up on that high ridge there sir!

Bullet HISS, blood splatters, distant GUNSHOT. A SOLDIER SCREAMS and falls
backwards clutching a gory wound.

French takes careful aim with his fifty caliber trapdoor rifle. BANG--BANG--BANG.
French watches as dust kicks up well in front of his target.

                             FRENCH
              Damn worthless rifle, can't hit a damn thing!

He tosses the rifle off to the side and stands up.

                             FRENCH
              Alright M Company. Set your sights for eight-
              hundred yards! And put a volley into that hill!
                     (beat)
              Fire!

GUNSHOTS. Dust kicks up from bullets hitting the ground near the distant dark
FIGURE.

                             FRENCH
              As you were! Back to your fighting positions!

                     OLD JOHN RYAN (V.O.)
              I think we put an end to that Indian, as there were
              no more men killed at that spot.

SOLDIERS scramble back to their cover. French exits. Ryan sees French's rifle
laying on the ground. He grabs it and wraps it up in a saddle blanket.

INT. TENT INTERVIEW - DAY

Walter Camp stops writing and looks up to Old Godfrey.

                          WALTER CAMP
              Did the Indians maintain any kind of intensity in
              their attacks?

                          OLD GODFREY
              Everybody was required to be on their bellies. The
              bullets came thick and fast.

                          WALTER CAMP
              And what about you?

OLD GODFREY

I kept moving about the lines even though it was
suggested I lie down too.

EXT. RENO HILL - DAY - MOMENTS LATER

Godfrey walks past SOLDIERS to FIRST SERGEANT DEWITT WINNEY.

OLD GODFREY (V.O.)

I was standing over Sergeant Winney when a bullet
went right through him.

Godfrey watches a bullet hit Winney. He falls back then slumps over grabbing a
bloody wound.

WINNEY

I'm hit!

Godfrey kneels next to Winney.

GODFREY

Lie down and be quiet! Soon as this ends, I'll have
you taken to the hospital.

WINNEY
(labored)
Yes sir!

Winney turns, then collapses dead.

OLD GODFREY (V.O.)

That's the first time since eighteen-sixty-one that I
had seen a man killed.

Godfrey watches Winney's dead body for several painful seconds.

INT. TENT INTERVIEW - DAY

Old Godfrey sits SILENT then turns to Walter Camp.

OLD GODFREY

A soldier begged me to lie down or I'd get hit, and
so I did. How I wished General Custer would
show up.

WALTER CAMP

Was there any talk of Custer?

                    OLD GODFREY
Captain Weir came over and we talked. It was my
opinion we ought to fold up the tents and silently
steal away. General Custer must surely be below us
and we could join him.

                    WALTER CAMP
Did you or Captain Weir raise this thought to
Major Reno?

                    OLD GODFREY
No. We both looked to Colonel Benteen to deliver
us from our situation.

                    WALTER CAMP
And why is that?

                    OLD GODFREY
It was our opinion that Colonel Reno didn't carry
the vigor to inspire our confidence.

Walter Camp stares momentarily to digest this thought, then scribbles feverishly.

EXT. TREES - DAY

Gall walks past a teepee into dense trees looking for his family.

                    WALTER CAMP (V.O.)
Those Indians who had their fill of blood for the
day returned to the Indian camp to take stock of
their own.

Battle SOUNDS are sporadic and very distant. Native materials are scattered on the
ground haphazardly.

He enters a clearing in the trees.

                    WALTER CAMP (V.O.)
                (tapers to morose and sad)
It was in a group of trees not far from the camp,
near the river, that Chief Gall found his entire
family...killed.

Strewn about the ground are the dead bodies of Gall Wives 1 & 2 and Gall Children
1, 2, & 3. He looks--stunned and shocked.

                    GALL
                (in Sioux)
Hiyá, hiyá, hiyá!
                    (MORE)

76

                    GALL (CONT'D)
                  (translation)
          No, no, no!

                OLD FOOLISH ELK (V.O.)
          The number of Indians killed in the battle was
          between thirty or forty.

He slowly walks over Gall Child 1's lifeless body. He kneels and picks her up. He
stammers then cries. He SCREAMS to the sky.

                OLD FOOLISH ELK (V.O.)
          Many more than this were wounded, and some
          died later.

He rocks her, sobbing uncontrollably. He caresses her hair then squeezes her tight.

                  WALTER CAMP (V.O.)
          The toll of war was felt by all that day.

INT. TENT INTERVIEW - DAY

Old Peter Thompson fumbles with his hat, Walter Camp looks up.

                OLD PETER THOMPSON
          We were becoming so tired of the Indians that
          they were no longer a terror to us.
                  (pause)
          The hill we were climbing seemed very long, so
          much so to me that I fell down and lay there with
          no inclination to move.

                  WALTER CAMP
          Is this near about you finding Major Reno?

                OLD PETER THOMPSON
          Watson called my attention to the head of the
          column of cavalry which came into plain view.

EXT. RENO HILL - AFTERNOON - LATER

Thompson and SOLDIER 5 emerge from a ravine and sprint towards SOLDIERS on
Reno Hill. Ryan watches.

                    RYAN
          C'mon, get on the hill!

OLD PETER THOMPSON (V.O.)
We were questioned closely as to what we knew
about Custer and we answered all as well as we
could.

GUNSHOTS. Thompson and Watson sprint past SOLDIERS and stop--winded.

Benteen walks up to Thompson and Watson. A bullet lands next to his foot. He looks then out to the distance.

BENTEEN
Pretty close call--try again!
            (to Thompson)
Who are you?

THOMPSON
Thompson, Company C sir. Our horses gave out on
General Custer's march to the north.

BENTEEN
For now, see to Lieutenant Mathey and secure the
pack mules!

THOMPSON
Yes sir!

Thompson and Watson exit.

The sun drops below the horizon. A golden cast of sunset befalls the land and quickly dims to pink.

INT. TENT INTERVIEW - DAY

Old Godfrey looks up to Walter Camp.

WALTER CAMP
How long did the fighting on the hill last?

OLD GODFREY
Till nearly dark, between nine and ten o'clock.

WALTER CAMP
Was there any inquiry about General Custer?

OLD GODFREY
Of course, everybody was wondering about him.

WALTER CAMP
And what was the opinion?

                    OLD GODFREY
I have to assume that most were of the belief that
he had been defeated and driven down the river
where he would probably join General Terry.

                    WALTER CAMP
And what of the night?

                    OLD GODFREY
The Indians were a good deal happier than we
were. All night long they continued their frantic
revels; beating tom-toms, dancing, whooping, and
yelling--bout drove men mad.

                                        CROSSFADE:

EXT. RENO HILL - NIGHT

Native CELEBRATIONS and MUSIC.

Godfrey sits staring out into the darkness--exhausted.

Thompson lays, his head propped on a saddle looking up at the crystal clear night sky--
exhausted.

                                        CROSSFADE:

INT. TENT INTERVIEW - DAY

Old Peter Thompson now sits in front of Walter Camp.

                    WALTER CAMP
The Indians were celebrating?

                    OLD PETER THOMPSON
By this time it was quite dark and I could plainly
see several large fires which the Indians had built.
The deep voices of the braves, the howling of the
squaws, the shrill of the children, and the barking
of the dogs made night hideous, but they appeared
to enjoy it amazingly.

                    WALTER CAMP
What did you do after this?

Old Peter Thompson looks up to Walter Camp.

                    OLD PETER THOMPSON
        I made my way to the place where my dead horse
        lay and stripped the saddle of everything and then
        went and made my bed behind my cracker box.

                    WALTER CAMP
        You were able to sleep?

EXT. RENO HILL - MORNING

                    OLD PETER THOMPSON (V.O.)
        I slept so soundly that I heard and knew nothing
        until I felt some one kicking the soles of my boots.

MAIN TITLE 24:
Reno Hill
June 26th, 1876,
Sunrise

Thompson lays sound asleep behind a saddle, his head on a rolled up great overcoat.
Benteen kicks his foot, his eyes open to Benteen standing over him.

                    BENTEEN
        Get the hell up now!

Thompson looks but Benteen's words are muted. SILENCE slowly gives way to
BATTLE SOUNDS.

                    BENTEEN
        C'mon, get up!

Thompson sits up and looks around--chaos, SOLDIERS running and SHOOTING.
Native WHOOPS and YELLS.

                    WALTER CAMP (V.O.)
        First light brought a sudden Indian surprise attack.
            (beat)
        An attack which threatened to overwhelm the
        entire command.

INT. TENT INTERVIEW - DAY

Old Peter Thompson stares at Walter Camp and pauses. Walter Camp looks up.

                    WALTER CAMP
        How bad was the situation?

Old Peter Thompson pauses, breathes, then looks distant.

> OLD PETER THOMPSON
> For the life of me I could not see how I could
> possibly get out of there alive for the bullets of the
> Indians were tearing up the ground in every
> direction

> OLD PETER THOMPSON (V.O.)
> The fire of the Indians seemed to come from three
> different directions and all exposed places were
> pretty well riddled.

INT. TENT INTERVIEW - DAY

Old John Ryan watches Walter Camp scribble.

> WALTER CAMP (V.O.)
> Would you say the situation was dire?

> OLD JOHN RYAN
> Captain Benteen's company was particularly hard
> pressed, and the men did their utmost to repulse
> those Indians.

> WALTER CAMP
> What did Captain Benteen do?

> OLD JOHN RYAN
> He called out to Major Reno for reinforcements,
> and my company was rushed to their assistance.

EXT. RENO HILL - MORNING - MOMENTS LATER

A bugle--"Charge" sounds.

ALL rise up and charge forward SCREAMING war cries. BANG--BANG--BANG.
WARRIORS watch and scatter left and right.

Thompson, Bennett, and Meador rush out, stop, and SHOOT their rifles.

WARRIORS SHOOT then fall back.

> THOMPSON
> (yelling)
> Yeah, you savages run for the hills!

Thompson reloads and SHOOTS his rifle.

A bullet hits Soldier 6 in the chest, he falls. SODLIERS run up and drag him backwards as he SCREAMS hysterically.

                        THOMPSON
            Get him outta here!

Soldier 5 hoists Soldier 6 up.

                        BENNETT
            Come on Thompson!

                        OLD PETER THOMPSON (V.O.)
            I had gotten so far without being hit that I thought
            I was going to get through safe, but as I was
            entering the mouth of the ravine a volley was fired
            by the Indians who occupied it and over I tumbled
            shot through the right hand and arm.

Thompson and Bennett run into the mouth of a ravine. They stop and SHOOT at WARRIORS. They SHOOT back.

                        OLD PETER THOMPSON
            A short distance away Benteen and several cavalry
            men, eleven in all; cleaned out that ravine held by
            so many Indians. They were resolute men.

A bullet hits Bennett in the back and he falls, Thompson grabs him. A bullet hits Thompson in the arm throwing him back--they crumple to the ground.

EXT. FIELD HOSPITAL - MORNING - MOMENTS LATER

                        OLD PETER THOMPSON (V.O.)
            I found in the center of our place of defense that
            we had a surgeon busily attending to the wounded
            and dying.

MAIN TITLE 25:
The Hospital
8:30 A.M.

                        WALTER CAMP (V.O.)
            Casualties filtered into the hospital from all fronts.

Doctor Porter maneuvers Thompson's sleeve, Thompson winces.

                        DOCTOR PORTER
            Looks like the bullet went up your arm and stuck.
            I won't be able to take it out here.

Doctor Porter bandages Thompson's wound.

> WALTER CAMP (V.O.)
> All the while Reno and Benteen led another set of
> charges in an effort to save the hill.

INT. TENT INTERVIEW - DAY

Old John Ryan looks momentarily lost in thought. Walter Camp looks up.

> WALTER CAMP
> Did you lose any men during this endeavor?

Ryan looks over to Walter Camp after several seconds.

> OLD JOHN RYAN
> Yes. Private James Tanner of my company was
> badly wounded. There was a call for volunteers, so
> I grabbed a blanket with three other men and
> rushed to his assistance.

EXT. FIELD HOSPITAL - MORNING - CONTINUOUS

COMMOTION--Doctor Porter looks.

Ryan and GROUP bring Tanner in. They lower him to the ground, Doctor Porter rushes over and treats a bloody chest wound.

> TANNER
> Please doc, I don't wanna die!

> DOCTOR PORTER
> You'll be ok. The bullet went through.

Doctor Porter's expression says otherwise. WOUNDED SOLDIERS watch. Tanner struggles to breathe.

> DOCTOR PORTER
> C'mon, stick with it now!

> TANNER
> I..I..

Tanner tries to speak but no words come out. He dies. Doctor Porter looks him over and checks for breathing. He throws the blood soaked bandages and rocks back into a seated position.

OLD JOHN RYAN (V.O.)
Only a few minutes after placing Tanner with the
rest of the wounded, he died.

Doctor Porter buries his head in his bloody hands. Ryan and GROUP watch.
Wounded Soldiers look away.

INT. TENT INTERVIEW - DAY

Walter Camp scribbles, stops, then looks up to Old Peter Thompson.

WALTER CAMP
What was the situation with water?

Old Peter Thompson looks to Walter Camp.

OLD PETER THOMPSON
As far as getting water was concerned it was a
matter of the greatest difficulty. All routes to the
river were cut off by the Indians.

EXT. FIELD HOSPITAL - MORNING - LATER

OLD PETER THOMPSON (V.O.)
I first found a man by the name of Bennett whom
to know was to respect. I could see that his days
were numbered.

Thompson walks around the field hospital looking left and right. WOUNDED
SOLDIER 3 clutches a terrible stomach wound SCREAMING.

MAIN TITLE 26:
A call for water
10:00 A.M.

WOUNDED SOLDIER 3
It hurts, it hurts so bad--please, please put me
down.

Thompson sees Bennett and kneels next him.

THOMPSON
Bennett, how ya doin'?

BENNETT
(labored and weak)
Terrible, just terrible.

84

                    THOMPSON
         Is there anythin' I can do for ya?

                    BENNETT
         Water Thompson, for the love God, water.

Thompson grabs a canteen, it's empty. He looks around--he sees the miserable faces of
WOUNDED SOLDIERS. He looks back to Bennett.

                    THOMPSON
         I'll bring water or I'll die tryin'

Bennett nods. Thompson exits.

                    OLD PETER THOMPSON (V.O.)
         I was determined to make the effort, and looked
         around for a canteen.

EXT. WATER CARRIER RAVINE - MORNING - MOMENTS LATER

                    WALTER CAMP (V.O.)
         You took it upon yourself to go alone?

                    OLD PETER THOMPSON (V.O.)
         Yes sir, as I went down the ravine I found it got
         narrower and deeper and became more lonesome
         and naturally more depressing.

Thompson walks down the last bit of a ravine then takes cover along a dirt out
cropping. He catches his breath. He nervously peers over the dirt pile and scans the
horizon.

                    OLD PETER THOMPSON (V.O.)
         I looked cautiously around the bend, and there
         before me was running water, the Little Bighorn
         River.

Only the sound of RUNNING WATER is heard. He looks over to the river, a small
strip of open ground is between him and the river.

                    OLD PETER THOMPSON (V.O.)
         I could see no signs of life and concluded to
         proceed.

EXT. RIVER - MORNING - CONTINUOUS

Thompson walks nervously to the river, drops his canteens, and awkwardly fills them
up with his one good hand using the canteen cup.

                              85

                    WALTER CAMP (V.O.)
          The trip to the river was done through some of
          the toughest terrain one can imagine, perhaps five-
          hundred yards of steep rocky gullies and sage.

He places each canteen over his shoulder then slowly moves back towards the ravine.

                    WALTER CAMP (V.O.) (CONT'D)
          And to fill one's cup or canteen was done so
          within plain eyesight of a massive Indian horde...
                         (beat)
          Thompson struggled through pain and agony to fill
          his canteens and then started the daunting task of
          scaling the hills from hence he came.

GUNSHOTS. A bullet hits Thompson in the head and he falls behind cover.

                    THOMPSON
          Ah, damnit!

He desperately dabs his head revealing blood. He looks up the ravine. It's a long ways.

                    THOMPSON
                    (to himself)
          Ah hell, just what have you gotten yourself into?

Thompson adjusts himself and runs a dead sprint up the ravine. GUNSHOTS--heavy BREATHING.

INT. TENT - DAY

A pen has stopped on the word came. PAUSE. Walter Camp resumes writing.

                    WALTER CAMP (V.O.)
          Despite being wounded twice and suffering from
          heat exhaustion, Private Thompson made it back
          to the lines.

EXT. FIELD HOSPITAL - MORNING - LATER

Thompson arrives with the canteens. He kneels next to Bennett and raises a canteen Bennett's lips.

                    THOMPSON
          Easy now.

Bennett drinks, WOUNDED SOLDIERS watch.

                              86

                    WOUNDED SOLDIER 4
Water! Water!

                    WOUNDED SOLDIER 5
Over here! Water over here! Please God man,
water!

WOUNDED SOLDIER 1 pulls out wadded money and holds it up.

                    WOUNDED SOLDIER 1
I'll give you ten dollars for a drink of water! Ten
dollars, good god man!

VOICES intermix into a chorus.

                         ALL
Water, we need water! Bring some over here!
Please!

                    WALTER CAMP (V.O.)
Hearing the commotion, Captain Benteen rushed
to the hospital area.

Benteen enters, Doctor Porter walks up to Benteen.

                       BENTEEN
What is going on here?

                    DOCTOR PORTER
The wounded need water sir. It's a medicine that is
in short supply.

Benteen looks to several of the WOUNDED SOLDIERS then back to Doctor Porter.

                       BENTEEN
I will get you more doctor.

Doctor Porter nods, Benteen exits.

                    OLD GODFREY (V.O.)
Up to this time, the command had been without
water.

INT. TENT INTERVIEW - DAY

                     OLD GODFREY
The excitement and heat made our thirst almost
maddening.

Walter Camp finishes writing and looks up.

> WALTER CAMP
> Round what time do you recall Benteen rousing
> volunteers?

> OLD GODFREY
> About 11 a-m. The firing was slack, and parties of
> volunteers formed to get water under the
> protection of Benteen's lines.

EXT. WATER CARRIER RAVINE - MORNING - MOMENTS LATER

Roy, Bancroft, PRIVATE AUGUSTUS DEVOTO, PRIVATE CHARLES
CAMPBELL, and eight WATER CARRIERS reach the valley floor behind dirt cover
and stop. ALL huff and PUFF out of breath.

> WALTER CAMP (V.O.)
> Perhaps it was divine intervention or perhaps luck,
> but the first few volunteers to go for water did so
> without a single shot fired over their heads.
> (dramatic pause)
> The eerie quiet did little to ease the men's minds.
> (beat)
> One by one each man made his trip to the river's
> edge.

They all look at the short distance between them and the river.

> ROY
> Alright, count off.

> BANCROFT
> Two.

> ALL
> (in turn say their number)
> Three, four.

> ROY
> (points to himself)
> Five.

> ALL (CONTD)
> Six, seven, eight, nine, ten, eleven, twelve.

> ROY
> When your number is called you can go in pairs or
> alone and however fast you see fit.

                                DEVOTO
              Sergeant, It might make for quicker work if we
              would fill the kettles up in the river and fill the
              canteens up here behind cover.

Roy nods.

                                 ROY
              That's not a half bad idea. Ok then, that's how it'll
              be done. Bancroft, shall we?

                              BANCROFT
              Let's get this done.

Bancroft and DeVoto grab the camp kettles and crouch run towards the river.

ALL keep watch from the dirt mound.

EXT. RENO HILL - MORNING - CONTINUOUS

Windolph watches the WATER CARRIERS hurry and scamper to the river and back.
He looks to Geiger who is aiming down the sights of his rifle.

                              WINDOLPH
              They ain't kicked the hornets nest yet. What are
              the Indians waitin; for?

                               GEIGER
              Got me beat. Let's hope they don't get wind of
              what we're up to.

EXT. RIVER - MORNING - CONTINUOUS

Bancroft and DeVoto stop, submerge the pots, and run back.

EXT. WATER CARRIER RAVINE - MORNING - CONTINUOUS

Bancroft and DeVoto scurry behind the mound and WATER CARRIERS pop
canteens open and begin filling them until the pots go dry.

                                 ROY
              Alright. Three, you're up!

A WATER CARRIER grabs a kettle and sprints to the river.

                                 ROY
              Four. Go!

                                  89

Another WATER CARRIER grabs a kettle and sprints off.

> OLD HE DOG (V.O.)
> We cut the Reno soldiers off and surrounded them
> on the high bluffs.

INT. TENT INTERVIEW - DAY

Old He Dog watches Walter Camp write.

> OLD HE DOG
> Later some soldiers went to river to get water.

Walter Camp scribbles, stops, and looks up.

> WALTER CAMP
> When you saw these soldiers, what did you do?

Old He Dog stares very seriously at Walter Camp.

> OLD HE DOG
> We shot at them.

EXT. WATER CARRIER RAVINE - MORNING - CONTINUOUS

> OLD HE DOG (V.O.)
> We tried to kill them, but we did not have time to
> do them all in.

He Dog and Standing Black Bear spot the Water Carriers, they quickly take aim and fire.

GUNSHOTS--a bullet hits Campbell in the shoulder. He drops his canteens and hobbles around.

EXT. RENO HILL - MORNING - CONTINUOUS

Geiger watches Roy and WATER CARRIERS help Campbell up the top of the ridge.

> GEIGER
> Three hundred on the sights men! Low in the
> brush on the far side of the river! Look for the
> smoke and let em have it!

BANG, BANG, BANG--Geiger and Windolph shoot as fast as they can reload.

> WALTER CAMP (V.O.)
> Equally commendable to those who ventured to
> the river were the few men who placed themselves
> at great risk to protect their comrades below.
> (beat)
> These men were some of the best shots the
> regiment could muster.

WARRIORS shoot back.

> OLD PETER THOMPSON (V.O.)
> My next trip to the river was taken with more
> courage.

INT. TENT INTERVIEW - DAY

Walter Camp writes as Old Peter Thompson looks distant.

> WALTER CAMP
> So Captain Benteen sent more volunteers to the
> river?

> OLD PETER THOMPSON
> Yes. I couldn't fire my rifle so I thought it a good
> idea to do my duty elsewhere.

> WALTER CAMP
> How many trips did you take to the river?

> OLD PETER THOMPSON
> Three total. They saw fit to award me a Medal of
> Honor for a day that'll be long remembered.

EXT. RENO HILL - MORNING - LATER

Thompson steps forward.

> THOMPSON
> Sir, I can't be any good with a rifle--my arm being
> this way, so I'll go.

PRIVATE WILLIAM SLAPER and PRIVATE MICHAEL MADDEN step forward.

> SLAPER
> Me and Madden, we'll go sir!

> BENTEEN
> Thank you Slaper.

Benteen turns to Roy.

                    BENTEEN
          Ok Sergeant, see to your men!

Benteen exits.

                    ROY
          Yes sir!
                    (turns)
          Thompson, Madden, Slaper trade off with those
          three there.

Roy, Thompson, Madden, Slaper, DeVoto, Bancroft, WATER CARRIERS exit down
the ravine.

EXT. WATER CARRIER RAVINE - MORNING - MOMENTS LATER

GUNSHOTS--WARRIORS SHOOT, SOLDIERS on the ridge SHOOT back.

                    WALTER CAMP (V.O.)
          The trips to the river continued most of the day.
          Time and time again, men risked their safety for a
          few handfuls of life saving water.

Roy, Thompson, Slaper, Madden, and eight WATER CARRIERS sprint down the
ravine as bullets kick dirt up around them. They crash into cover behind the dirt
mound at the bottom of the ravine.

                    ROY
          Drop the canteens in a pile here, and pass the
          kettles up!

ALL drop their canteens and pass the kettles and pots forward.

                    ROY
          Just like before. We'll count off and go to the river
          in turn with the kettles then back as quick as you
          can.

ALL nod.

                    ROY
          Madden, Thompson, and Slaper, y'all hang back a
          couple runs to get a feel for it. I'll go first, one.

92

                         ALL
                      (in turn)
Two, three, four, five, six, seven, eight, nine, ten,
eleven, twelve.

                         ROY
Alright, move!

ALL SHOOT, Bancroft sprints towards the river. Madden scoots forward, waits,
takes off running.

A bullet hits him in the leg and he falls hard to the ground. He SCREAMS.

Bancroft runs from the river, sees Madden, and stops.

                      BANCROFT
Ah Christ! Stay down in cover and we'll come
back for ya.

                      MADDEN
Just git outta here!

Madden GRUNTS and GROANS and pulls himself along back towards Roy.

Bancroft ducks into cover.

                      BANCROFT
Sergeant Roy, Madden got hit in the leg by the
river. It looks bad.

Roy looks out and sees Madden crawling.

                         ROY
                      (shouting)
Keep comin' Madden, we'll get ya!
                      (turns)
Thompson you're up, go!

Thompson dashes out, men reload pistols and fill canteens--GUNSHOTS WHIP and
CRACK overhead. Thompson trips, falls, and slides next to Madden.

He Dog and Standing Black Bear shoot.

                      THOMPSON
Madden!

                      MADDEN
I'm alright, get the water and get goin'!

Thompson nods and exits. Madden painfully drags himself closer and closer to Roy. Two WATER CARRIERS run out and help drag him the rest of the way. Madden SCREAMS and MOANS through the whole process.

Roy props Madden up against the dirt mound and pulls Madden's boot off. Blood rolls thick on the ground.

                    ROY
          Oh God!

                    MADDEN
          I'll be aight!

Thompson returns.

                    ROY
          That's it. Finish off the canteens and let's get outta
          here!

WATER CARRIERS close their canteens and sling them over their shoulders.

                    MADDEN
          Don'tcha be worryin' bout me. I'll be alright, I'll
          be safe here.

                    ROY
          To hell with that!
               (turns)
          You all, help me carry Madden!

Bancroft, Slaper, and three others help Roy hoist Madden up.

                    ROY
          The rest of ya, git to the top--go!

ALL move back up the ravine as fast as they can. Heavy GUNSHOTS.

                    WALTER CAMP (V.O.)
          There were casualties?

INT. TENT INTERVIEW - DAY

Walter Camp looks up to Old Godfrey.

                    OLD GODFREY
          Several men were wounded. The Indians were in
          the brush and woods and opened fire whenever a
          man exposed himself, which made this a
          particularly hazardous service.

94

WALTER CAMP
Were there efforts to get the wounded back to the
lines?

OLD GODFREY
Yes. This of course incurred additional danger, and
I believe all those men were rewarded with Medals
of Honor.

EXT. FIELD HOSPITAL - DAY - MOMENTS LATER

Roy and GROUP bring Madden in to the field hospital.

ROY
Got another one doc!

They lay Madden down as gently as they can. Doctor Porter rushes over and looks
over the leg wound. He turns to Roy.

DOCTOR PORTER
That'll be all soldier, thank you!

ROY
Yes sir!

Roy and GROUP leave their canteens and exit. Madden MOANS as Doctor Porter
probes the wound.

MADDEN
How bad is it doc?

DOCTOR PORTER
The bone is shattered, I'm gonna have to amputate
the leg. I'm sorry.

Madden looks away and GROANS. Doctor Porter lays the tools out to amputate
Madden's leg. Doctor Porter props a bottle of brandy next to his medical instruments.

DOCTOR PORTER
Here take a swift pull on this to brace yourself up.

Doctor Porter uncorks the bottle and raises it to Madden's mouth and he takes a big
gulp from it. He swishes it around and swallows.

WALTER CAMP (V.O.)
Brandy was about the only anesthetic available
that day.

Doctor Porter turns to two WOUNDED SOLDIERS.

DOCTOR PORTER

You two, you ain't hurt so bad. Come here and
help me.

Wounded Soldiers move each beside Madden.

DOCTOR PORTER

Now you hold him tight case he gets to buckin'.
     (to Madden)
Bite down on this.

Doctor Porter places a stick wrapped in cloth in Madden's teeth. His breathing
increases nervously.

WALTER CAMP (V.O.)

     (dark, blunt and matter of fact)
Before the times of modern medicine, soldiers in
battle finding themselves wounded in the arms or
legs would almost certainly find those afflicted
limbs being removed at the closest joint.

Doctor Porter tightens the tourniquet, he grabs the bone saw and pauses.

Madden looks at Doctor Porter.

MADDEN

     (with the stick in his mouth)
Just get it done doc.

Doctor Porter nods and saws into Madden's leg. Disgusting SAWING SOUNDS.

Madden squirms and GROANS and SCREAMS. The saw cuts through the last bit of
Madden's legs. Doctor Porter removes the severed limb and wraps up the stump.

Madden BREATHES heavily and spits the stick out. Doctor Porter raises the bottle
of brandy up to Madden's mouth and gives him another drink.

Madden smacks his lips and smirks.

MADDEN

Doc, for another pull of that stuff and you can cut
off my other leg.

WALTER CAMP (V.O.)

Private Madden would go on to survive the battle
and later be promoted to Sergeant by his
commander, Lieutenant Godfrey.

ALL CHUCKLE. Madden's body relaxes back into the ground as Doctor Porter
wraps his bloody stump.

WALTER CAMP (V.O.)
What, would you say, were the condition of the
men?

Madden passes out.

INT. TENT INTERVIEW - DAY

Old Varnum continues looking distant as if he is no longer there.

OLD VARNUM
Young boys quickly became old men, laying in
trenches beside bloated and rotting corpses, but
fought like old veterans of years' standing.

Walter Camp stops writing, looks up, and both pause to digest this information.

WALTER CAMP
Did anyone try and carry a message out?

Old Varnum looks over to Walter Camp.

OLD VARNUM
I propositioned Major Reno to let me leave the
lines if someone would go with me.

EXT. RENO HILL - DAY - CONTINUOUS

OLD VARNUM (V.O.)
I thought at night I could get through the lines and
carry our fix to any troops I could reach.

Reno sits behind ammo and bread boxes, beat and tired. Varnum approaches and
kneels.

VARNUM
Sir, I'd like to volunteer to try and get a message
out to Gen'l Terry.

Reno looks around in momentary thought.

VARNUM
Sir?

Reno looks back to Varnum

RENO
We can't afford to lose two good shots and you'd
probably be killed anyways.

Varnum is disappointed.

                    VARNUM
          We might as well get killed trying to get relief as to
          get killed where we are.

                    RENO
          Varnum, you are a very uncomfortable companion.
          The request is denied.

                    OLD VARNUM (V.O.)
          He later agreed to let the Scouts try and get word
          out.

Varnum hesitates as if to say something then exits. Reno shakes his head.

                    WALTER CAMP (V.O.)
          So the Indian village, it broke up following the
          fight?

INT. TENT INTERVIEW - DAY

Old He Dog stares at Walter Camp.

                    OLD HE DOG
          After the fight, all tribes went up river near to Big
          Hills.

                    WALTER CAMP
          Did you stay together?

                    OLD HE DOG
          All remained together until got to Slim Buttes.
          They split up after that, Sitting Bull set out for
          Canada. Had assistance not come to the soldiers on
          the high hills, we would have killed them all.

EXT. RIVER - DAY - CONTINUOUS

                    WALTER CAMP (V.O.)
          How many Indians died?

Sitting Bull stands motionless near the edge of the Little Big Horn River
contemplating the last couple days.

> OLD HE DOG (V.O.)
> The number of Indians killed was between thirty
> and forty. Many more than this were wounded,
> and some died later.

INT. TENT INTERVIEW - DAY

Walter Camp finishes writing and looks up to Old John Ryan.

> WALTER CAMP
> Was there any other fighting of note you recall of
> that day?

> OLD JOHN RYAN
> On a high bluff some distance away, the Indians
> put in a few good shots which laid us all low.

EXT. SHARPSHOOTER RIDGE - DAY - MOMENTS LATER

WARRIOR SNIPER lays low to the ground, his body camouflaged slightly by a deer
hide covering him. The long barrel of a fifty caliber Sharps rifle sticks through the
antlers of a bison skull.

He takes careful aim at very distant shadowy SOLDIERS on Reno Hill.

EXT. RENO HILL - DAY - CONTINUOUS - INTERCUT

A bullet hits a SOLDIER, distant GUNSHOT, he falls wounded. SOLDIERS
scramble to pull him to cover. French raises his binoculars towards a large hill, puff of
smoke.

Another SOLDIER falls wounded. French drops the binoculars.

> FRENCH
> Ryan! Can you get that pesky Indian up there with
> that rifle of yours there?

Ryan looks out--very distant and sees a puff of smoke, bullet CRACKS, distant
GUNSHOT.

> RYAN
> It's a hell of a shot but I'll get to work sir!

> FRENCH
> Alright then.
> (turns)
> Keep your bits in the dirt or they'll get shot off.

99

Ryan props his rifle up on a rolled blouse. He flips his sight up and sets his sight at 500 yards. He SHOOTS and watches where the dirt kicks up.

He adjusts his sights and SHOOTS again then makes more adjustments. He lays several cartridges next to him so that he can reload rapidly.

                    WALTER CAMP (V.O.)
          What effect did your shots have on the Indians?

He cocks the hammer, takes careful aim, clicks the second trigger, then places his finger on the main trigger, BANG. He reloads, BANG, reloads, BANG.

                    OLD JOHN RYAN (V.O.)
               (chuckles)
          Those Indians scampered away, and that ended
          their firing in a most memorable engagement.

Dirt kicks up next to Warrior Sniper, then a bullet CRACK, dust kicks up again. Warrior Sniper runs away.

Ryan watches and waits. No more puffs. SOLDIERS CHEER.

EXT. RENO HILL - DAY - LATER

                    WALTER CAMP (V.O.)
          What can you say of the actions of the officers
          during the battle?

Weary eyed SOLDIERS watch the ridges but see nothing. An odd QUIET fills the air, only the gentle rush of LIGHT WINDS and PRAIRIE AMBIENCE are heard.

                    OLD JOHN RYAN (V.O.)
          Major Reno and Captain Benteen, in fact all the
          officers, did all they could in order to defeat the
          Indians.

MAIN TITLE 27:
Reno Hill
3:00 P.M.

Benteen kneels with Reno watching the valley. He sees in the distance a dust cloud obscuring thousands of NATIVES leave creating a dust cloud a mile high.

He turns to Reno.

                    BENTEEN
          It seems our savage friends have grown tired and
          have left us.

100

                              RENO
          One can only hope.

The dust clears slightly and Reno's face turns to shock.

                              RENO
          There must be some eight-thousand Indians down
          there.

                              BENTEEN
          Jesus, it looks like a division worth of em.

                              SOLDIER 8
          They're leavin'!

SOLDIERS stand and CHEER! They wave their hats, weapons--anything in their
hands.

INT. TENT INTERVIEW - DAY

Walter Camp scribbles in his book and then looks up.

                              WALTER CAMP
          Did you have any inclination as to why they
          decided to leave?

                              OLD GODFREY
          We thought maybe Custer had gotten to Terry, or
          perhaps they were short on ammunition. There
          was even the rumor it was a ruse to get us to move
          then they'd clean us out.

                              WALTER CAMP
          What did you think?

                              OLD GODFREY
          I thought...thank God.

EXT. RENO HILL - EVENING

                              WALTER CAMP (V.O.)
          How many casualties did you incur?

Godfrey watches SOLDIERS drag and carry DEAD SOLDIERS and roll them into
pits with other DEAD SOLDIERS.

                                101

> OLD GODFREY (V.O.)
> Our loss on the hill had been eighteen killed and
> fifty-two wounded.

WOUNDED SOLDIERS are revealed in varying manners of despair and suffering.

> OLD GODFREY (V.O.)
> General Custer and all five companies under his
> command, some two-hundred ten men, would be
> found and buried the next day.

Waving grass against a cloud filled blue sky.

EXT. RENO HILL - SUNSET

The red orange sky of late evening silhouettes SOLDIERS sitting and standing on the ridge of Reno Hill. Other SOLDIERS throw dirt on top of dead bodies.

> WALTER CAMP (V.O.)
> Reno and Benteen's battle worn soldiers were
> rescued the following day with the arrival of
> General Alfred Terry's forces.

One SOLDIER walks up and places his hand on the shoulder of another SOLDIER to comfort him.

> CROSSFADE:

INT. TENT INTERVIEW - DAY

Walter Camp sits alone scribbling his words feverishly into his notebook.

> WALTER CAMP (V.O.)(CONT'D)
> And the Native Warriors who won the battle
> would be hunted..hounded..and harassed for the
> next fourteen years.
> (beat)
> Until they had no will left to fight.

Walter Camp stops, breathes, then scribbles more.

> WALTER CAMP (V.O.)
> As for the cause of Custer's defeat. We might
> never know.

He finishes writing and sets his pencil down and closes his book.

> FADE TO BLACK.

EPILOGUE TITLE 1.
The 7th U.S. Cavalry lost 268 soldiers, scouts, government employees, and civilians.

                    WALTER CAMP (V.O.)
          The Seventh U.S. Cavalry lost two-hundred sixty
          eight soldiers, scouts, government employees, and
          civilians.

EPILOGUE TITLE 2.
Many could not be identified and remain "unknown".

                    WALTER CAMP (V.O.)
          Many could not be identified and remain unknown.

EPILOGUE TITLE 3.
At least 68 Native American Warriors, women, and children died.

                    WALTER CAMP (V.O.)
          At least sixty eight Native American Warriors,
          women, and children died.

EPILOGUE TITLE 4.
The true total may never be known.

                    WALTER CAMP (V.O.)
          The true total may never be known.

EPILOGUE TITLE 5:
24 Medals of Honor were awarded for bravery during the battle.

                    WALTER CAMP (V.O.)
          Twenty four Medals of Honor were awarded for
          bravery during the battle.

EPILOGUE TITLE 6:
It would take 127 years for the Native American participants to receive any
recognition for their bravery and sacrifice.

                    WALTER CAMP (V.O.)
          However, it would take one-hundred twenty-
          seven years for the Native American participants
          to receive any recognition for their bravery and
          sacrifice.

EPILOGUE TITLE 7.
This film is dedicated to the memory of all those who fought and died at the Little
Big Horn.

WALTER CAMP (V.O.)
This film is dedicated to the memory of all those
who fought and died at the Little Big Horn.

DEDICATION TITLE 2:
In Memoriam
Thomas R. Eastman - Friend, historian, and Executive Producer
Helori M. Graff - Friend and Executive Producer
Stevan E. Peckel - Friend, historian, and Associate Producer
Gerry Schultz - Friend, historian, and researcher.

THE END

Appendix 1

One Lonely Tombstone (an introspective view of the battle from the author)

The heat is sweltering. A bead of sweat runs down a young soldier's brow, smearing the dirt and powder residue on his cheek. A light breeze ruffles his scruffy, unkempt brown hair. Those typically brown eyes that had often shined at the life he'd lived thus far were now intense and scared. Gunfire erupts from the left. He looks. Several hundred Indian braves smash into a thin blue line of cavalry soldiers. His eyes track left to the far right; smoke, dust, rugged Earth, and death. His pupils constrict. At this moment, he realizes that this is the fight of his life. He is only 20 years old. He pulls a rifle cartridge from his pistol belt; it fumbles and falls. The gleaming sun reflects on the copper sheen as it gracefully spins in the air on its way downward. It hits the ground, rebounding until it rests peacefully in a pile of fired casings. Rolling smoke obscures the land, and the details fade away to the annuals of time.

Near today's Hardin, Montana, along the Little Bighorn River's quiet waters, on June 25, 1876, a dust cloud lifted late in the afternoon, revealing the apocalyptic carnage of over 200 dead, stripped, and mutilated bodies. This nightmarish visage became enshrined with white marble tombstones. The tombstones "mark" where each soldier fell; they are called markers because of that. These same markers whirred past my window as I drove by. The golden mid-day sun cast an orange glow on my Army camouflage cap, Shemagh, pro-military t-shirt, and blue jeans. I was in between film shoots for a local battle reenactment group, so I decided to pay my respects. I parked in a pull out along the road and exited my vehicle. I stood at the edge of the pavement--almost like an invisible boundary, and leaned forward as far as my body would allow thinking that being just a few inches closer would help my understanding. Clusters of these lonely memorials spider web out in the directions these men ran in the final frantic moments of their life. It was coincidentally June 25 when I found myself near a place known as the "swale." My gaze panned a field painted red with the blood that time and the elements had long washed away, ingesting the hell that had descended on this locale.

'What a place to die,' I thought.

A soldier can always understand the life of another soldier. I was a 14 year Army veteran, and I, too, saw combat, having been to Iraq twice and Afghanistan once. I know the violence that man can do to one another. Being in battle, I was always comforted knowing that my brothers would watch over me and keep me safe and, if need be, save me, as would I. Was it the same for these men? War never seems to change, just the uniforms, weapons, and technology. These men, too, must have felt that bond. This battle, the final resting place of 210 men, resonated with me on a very personal level because of my intimate understanding of the military lifestyle.

A Park Service Ranger in a nicely pressed brown and tan uniform asked me, "Would you like to go down, sir?"

As if telling Santa what I wanted for Christmas, I responded, "Yes. I would love to."

Another volunteer, an older lady whose clothes were adorned with Custer pin on memorabilia, smiled and led me down a well-beaten path paralleling several individual markers and ends in a vast collection at the bottom of a depression sliced in two by a ravine. She plopped down a simple folding chair at the end of the path and sat down. I stood there, peering at all the white marble markers clumped together. They must have fought and died back to back and shoulder to shoulder. They shouldn't be there, but they were. This place was a culmination of what we like to call "Murphy's Law." Murphy's Law states, "everything that can go wrong, will." I took out my camera phone and snapped a picture. I shifted my point of aim to another set of tombstones and imagined this place 100 years from now.

The thick brush has almost masked the markers in untrimmed buffalo grass and sagebrush. It hasn't changed much. Tourists still flock by the hundreds of thousands a year to look at this dark spot on U.S. history and pour over the details that will always be unknown. They, too, snap pictures with their new-age cameras and post them on the social media equivalents to come.

Lowering my camera I thought, 'would anyone ever stand in a place where I was in combat and take pictures, imagining my face as I drug wounded and dead soldiers off the battlefields in the Middle East?' I suppose not. What of these young fellows here? They would have been looking and shooting there, a ridge on the right. On the left, a ravine; they would have fired again as more warriors came to count coup and defend their village. Thomas Patrick Downing was a soldier who died that day, probably not far from where I was standing. He is merely one person of the faceless hundreds that died that day, but for me, he is a symbol representative of all the "unknown" markers littering the field.

The weather and temperature were very close to the battle that day: hot, dry, and miserable. Wiping the sweat from my forehead, I found my ear turning like a radar dish searching for stimulation. It was dead silent. As if peeling back a layer that was otherwise muffling the real world, I could hear the gentle kiss of a very light breeze and the distant singing of day crickets. This silence was unnerving, unsettling. I found my mind wandering beyond the realm of reality. Feeling I might be attacked from all directions without notice, I turned a full 360 degrees. There were no cars, no houses, no roads, and no amber waves of neatly planted grain. It was at this moment that I became self-aware of the vista these men last saw. It was desperately picturesque and violently beautiful. Besides myself, the volunteer, and the tombstones, it was as close to 1876 that you could get. For a moment, I imagined myself there.

BANG, BANG, chaos. Riderless horses thunder past me. I see him, Thomas. He steps back, his foot trips over the leg of a fallen comrade, and he collapses to the rear. Momentarily he locks eye contact with the recently departed, a man he played cards with often, blood oozes from a chest wound. I stand over Thomas as he kicks himself backward. The Indian horde crests the horizon. I reach down to help him, but he is not there, a figment of my imagination. I am wrapped in a nightmare that I seemingly cannot wake from, and it feels real—my heart races. I'm left helpless, only there to bear witness to the inevitable fact that Thomas will die with the rest of these men.

The war-whoops drown out all other sounds except for the sporadic gunfire.

Thomas loads a round into his 1873 Springfield carbine, BANG! A single Indian falls from his horse. He reloads, BANG! The black powder smoke seems suffocating.

Claustrophobia sets in, the world view narrows. Thirty of us are surrounded. The horde washes over us like a red tidal wave, drowning us in our blood. The image is too much to bear, and my solemn grimace redirects to Thomas kneeling at the end of this blue line. He watches as the dust from hundreds more Indians speed over the next ridge. His facial expression reflects the direness of the situation. Time is running out. Those now left flee as wholesale slaughter intermixes with the rank and file. Their faces are stricken with intense panic. An arm grabs Thomas' shoulder and hoists him up. He looks, his shocked gaze falling onto a dusty silhouette shaking him.

"Get to Custer," the faceless shadow shouts and then takes off as if he never missed a stride in stopping for Thomas.

Custer is a far ways back and on the other side of the ridge. Another set of violent gunshots go off, behind me now. My gaze shifts to a cloud of smoke and dust on the horizon, not too far away. Custer is engaged. I look back; Thomas is in full flight; over my shoulder, the horde approaches. Instinct takes over, and I follow Thomas. He casts his heavy rifle aside as if the extra weight will slow him down and sprints at a heart attack pace towards the top of a ridge. For a moment, it all feels ok. He looks back to see the bloody debacle fast approaching as those men slower than him fall like buffalo during a hunt.

Tomahawks swing. Arrows WHISTLE. Bullets CRACK. The blood sprays red, pooling in mass around the dark blue figures on the ground. He huffs, his lungs burn, the sweat is now pouring down like a waterfall. He can see his final destination, and it is only a short sprint away. There is still hope.

WHACK! Thomas tries moving his feet, but they are not cooperating. A searing pain develops high on his back, but he cannot see it. An arrow is sticking out from between his shoulder blades. He tries to keep pace, but his legs give out. He collapses into a dusty patch of sage and dirt.

The pain is grotesque, not like anything he's ever felt before. He claws and scratches his way forward. His screams echo and reverberate through the landscape. The tidal wave of death approaches, dissipating into a lone ghostlike warrior on horseback galloping in slow motion. Time slows. Every breath is labored and acute—the strike of the horse's hooves crash like thunder. The war-whoops become unworldly fodder, bombarding the eardrums. Fear and panic saturate Thomas's senses. A war club momentarily silhouettes against the blinding sun. It swings down, black.

I want to look away, but I can't. Thomas's bloody image disappears, replaced by one lonely tombstone with the inscription "U.S. SOLDIER 7th CAVALRY FELL HERE JUNE 25 1876." There is no way of knowing where Thomas, or any of the other unnamed soldiers, died explicitly, just that they did. The desolation of the marker brought a flood of emotions to my heart as I looked back to where I had only been. A large grouping of white headstones thinning out to this spot, and then, nothing. The emotion I felt wasn't in this single marker but in the idea that washed over me as to who this gentleman must have been. Indeed in life, he had a name? In death, he now remains nameless.

The depressive feelings of who this gentleman might have been caught me off guard. It was at that moment, standing there next to a single monument which collectively made up the entire story of human travesty, that I began to see the desperation of it all; to understand the scope of this place. A soldier should never die alone. A soldier who dies in battle should not be unknown; however, it is a governing theme on this hallowed ground. I envisioned who this man might have been before all this. Maybe he wasn't that much different than me. Perhaps he had a wife, kids, and aspirations. Perishing in combat, alone and forgotten, is anguish I could never truly contemplate; but 139 years ago, there a soldier laid; scared, dying, and alone.

Appendix 2

On Reno and Benteen at the Little Big Horn

The first thing I always point out to students of this battle is that you have the luxury of hindsight. You have at your disposal over 140 years of research, testimony, archeological evidence, myth, legends, and hearsay. On the ground at the Little Big Horn on June 25, 1876, the guys had no such luxuries. The extent of their knowledge extended to only what they could see or hear, and they acted on instinct, training, and orders. One also must not forget that the fog of war is real; for you, it might be clear, for them, it was not. Keep this in mind throughout the following text.

This battle was supremely complex, with thousands of moving pieces to consider at any one time. One of the reoccurring themes I see in my studies is a constant need to "blame" or "shame" various participants to pinpoint a reason for the battle's outcome. It is not that simple. Lieutenant Colonel George A. Custer, Major Marcus Reno, and Captain Frederick Benteen were fascinating characters. Each man had their own strengths ad weaknesses, and there absolutely existed a good deal of friction between them. A very lengthy conversation could be had on the varying personalities of the 7th Cavalry alone, but this text will only focus on the elements of these relationships that are relevant to this reading.

Postulating that Custer failed to achieve any desirable outcome because his subordinate commanders failed him isn't a new theory. It's been an ongoing debate since June 27, 1876. Yes, personality conflicts existed between the commanders in the 7th cavalry, but you must also remember that these officers were professional career soldiers. They acted as such when it mattered, and it certainly mattered in battle. No officer wanted to see the command or campaign fail to achieve their objectives. It is this pursuit of a mutual endgame that united these characters. At no time would Lieutenant Colonel Custer, Major Reno, or Captain Benteen knowingly jeopardize the operation.

Let's jump into this analysis, which begins at the end of Benteen's scout to the left.

Benteen more than likely ended his scout faster than Custer anticipated he would have. He got to that last bluff along his line of march and believed that continuing was pointless. The horses were wearing out, there was nothing ahead of him except an endless visage of rugged hills, and they had lost sight of the valley and the command, so he made a command decision to find the command's trail to reunite with the regiment. Some will argue that Benteen was deliberately slow on this march. This thinking completely ignores the timed studies that have been done along Benteen's purported route. This thinking also ignores the terrain and the size of his battalion, which dictated how fast he could move at any given time. From the moment he ended his scout and moved towards Reno Creek, he made excellent time as he moved to the morass.

It's also postulated that Benteen needlessly delayed at the morass, but this again ignores apparent factors. His battalion of horses was wearing thin, and it took time for the three companies to cycle through the water supply. It was a morass, not a long flowing river where an entire company could spread out and let the horses drink. It took time to execute, and those without intimate military experience often don't realize that things in the military--logistics--take time. Incorporating military logistics into the conversation will become more apparent through this reading.

Benteen and his men could hear firing to the north, and at this point, it would have been from Reno's fight in the valley. Most of the argument for Benteen wasting time at the morass seems to be due in part to Captain Thomas Weir's impatience. Weir's company was the first to cycle through the watering of the horses, filling of canteens, and he didn't want to wait any longer. I will reiterate that the moment's logistics dictated how much time was necessary to complete the watering task. After a spat with Benteen, Weir left without orders and moved on. To show just how little impact this impatient move had on Benteen's battalion, Weir moved out approximately 15 minutes before the rest of the battalion. Benteen caught up with him in almost the same amount of time—that's pretty fast by horse standards.

Benteen didn't needlessly waste time at the morass. His time spent there was an absolute military logistical necessity.

Neither man nor horse had water since the night before, and the size of the morass dictated how fast this operation could be completed. His gait before and after the morass was at slow gallop speeds, so he certainly was not lingering on the march.

Near the morass, Benteen encountered Sergeant Daniel Kanipe, who proclaimed to be carrying a message to Captain Thomas McDougall for the pack train. Kanipe was cited as saying, "they had them on the run." This general comment appears to have had some effect on the men present, giving a false presumption that everything was going better than planned with Custer's operation to the north. So strong was this idea that Lieutenant Edward Godfrey penned in his diary that they thought "all that was left was to go up and congratulate the others."

Shortly after that, Benteen encountered Private Giovani Martini, who passed the famous "last note" and likewise alluded that the fighting to the north was in hand. Martini was cited as telling Benteen the Indians were "skedaddling." It's important to note that Martini later denied saying these words, so it cannot be known with all certainty that he uttered them. Still, we cannot merely dismiss it. Given that Benteen mentioned several times in his accounts that this is what he had been told, if true, then this would further reinforce the idea that all was in hand. This doesn't mean that they were lulled into complacency--perhaps a false sense of security, but not to the point of dereliction. They heard the firing ahead, so they knew the game was still afoot.

Before going further, we have to also look at the note Martini carried. This message is probably one of the most ambiguous aspects of the battle because it is, in fact, the last words from Custer that can be confirmed with all certainty. "Benteen. Come on. Big villag (sic). Be quick. Bring pack (sic). W. W. Cook (sic) & bring pack (sic)." So here's where it gets a bit convoluted, and Michael Donahue recently talked about this very much in detail. For the longest time, the message was interpreted as "Benteen. Come on. Big village. Be quick. Bring packs. P.S. Bring pack (sic). W. W. Cooke." You can see the subtle differences between the original writing and the later accepted version. Lieutenant W. W. Cooke was a very lazy writer. He often left letters off the end of words, even his name.

It has been interpreted this way forever because of Benteen's handwritten text at the top of the note. Just a few fun facts there, but let's break the message down in the way the military would interpret it in the day:

Come on = change of mission, and can be translated as "your scout is no longer necessary, move your battalion forward."

Big village = an intelligence update, and can be translated as "we have ascertained the village's size and position."

Be quick = speed, and can be translated as "move at as a rapid a gait as you deem prudent."

Bring pack = an order, and can be translated a couple of ways. Either it means "break out the packs from the mules and advance them forward," or and probably more likely, "ensure the pack train is continually moving forward without delay."

Bring pack (2nd use) = emphasis or clarity of the previous order, and is interpreted the same. Cooke might very well have added the second "bring pack" because his first "bring pack" was so lazily written, and he was clarifying his words.

Past and present, too many tend to read entirely too much into this note, given its simplicity. In military terms, here is how the message would have probably been interpreted on June 25, 1876:

Benteen. We have located the village, and your scout is no longer necessary. Move your battalion forward at as rapid a gait as you deem prudent and ensure the pack train moves without delay.

Pretty simple right? The famous last note was merely a means to start consolidating the command to support the attack that was now in action. Given the note's brevity and vagueness, Benteen could also have reasonably expected additional orders when he and the pack train met the intent of the orders.

Unfortunately, no follow-up orders came, so we are left with just the simple words scribbled hastily on a piece of paper.

To validate my conclusions, you only need to compare the note to other orders issued that day:

Custer to Benteen when sending him on the scout to the left, "I want you to proceed to that line of bluffs and pitch into anything you come across." Custer later sent two additional follow on orders to Benteen, "if you find nothing on reaching the second line of bluffs, you are to continue on with the same instructions," and "if after the third line of bluffs you find nothing and can see the valley to pitch into it."

Custer's orders to Reno via Cooke, "Major Reno, the village is just ahead and running away. The general wishes for you to advance your companies forward at as rapid a gait as you deem prudent and attack the village at once. The entire command will support you."

So you can see how deliberately and specifically Custer issued orders that day. Had Custer intended a specific set of instructions from the last note, they would have been dictated that way verbally and in writing. This was also the only message that was written during the battle, and this was due in part to Martini's lack of English speaking capabilities.

This leads to the next factoid. Martini was not next in line to carry a message. Per Martini, Trumpeter Henry Dose was, in fact, next in line to take a message. Dose had no English issues and would have been the right man if specific instructions needed to be passed. Cooke called on Dose to carry this message, but Custer interjected and told Cooke to send Martini because "Martini knows Benteen." If this message was supercritical and specific to Custer's plans, why would he personally interject to send what could be argued as the worst possible messenger for the job? The reasoning is straightforward; they were simple orders. The intent was for Benteen and the pack train to get moving towards the fight to support the ongoing attack.

Some continue to argue that part of the last note intended for Benteen to come directly to Custer. This shows a lack of understanding of Custer's M.O. and how the situation developed up to this point. Custer didn't mince words. If Custer wanted Benteen to come directly to him, he would have said it specifically, especially when it came to Benteen. The second point of order is the disposition and separation of units on the battlefield. Custer would have known that Benteen wasn't aware of where the other battalions were, so he would need to give more explicit orders to Benteen if he wanted such a specific move to be made. No such specifics were given, and the general philosophy of separated units during this time period is to "move to the sound of the guns." So without instructions to the contrary, Benteen would continue to move towards Reno regardless.

Now that we understand Benteen's orders and the overall picture of his mission at hand, we can move on to meeting Reno. Benteen ran into some scouts who made mention of soldiers on a hill, and he changed course to meet what he thought was the entire regiment. We must remember that Benteen had no idea who or what was where, so it was purely logical to move forward with the packs as instructed and do so to the first available parts of the regiment he found. He then could then seek out additional orders if they weren't delivered to him sooner. This is how Benteen ran into Reno's beaten battalion on the heights, and this is when the gravity of the situation began to settle in. He learned that Reno had been beaten back, half his unit was dead or missing, and no one knew where Custer was.

Now we need to address a few items that frequently come up in regards to Benteen at this moment during the battle:

He beat the pack train to the hill by almost an hour, and you have to remember that his orders involved both he and the pack train moving forward. A task he was accomplishing.

He had no additional instructions on where to go or what to do beyond the above, so he would have exercised his discretion to achieve that intent.

Reno became the ranking officer once Benteen reunited with the regiment. Benteen had no specific orders that would overturn Reno's rank or authority. This was the military, there was a chain of command, and it very much followed strict etiquette in those days.

It was at this time that Reno asked Benteen to "halt his command and help," that "He (Reno) had lost half his command." Reno was now the senior officer, so Benteen had a moral and lawful responsibility to follow Reno's requests and orders. To make a special note, Benteen at no time hid behind Reno's rank—that flies right in the face of Benteen's persona. If given the option, I believe Benteen would have opted to be out on his own in command of a battalion rather than play second fiddle to Reno. Benteen showed Reno the note, and they did start to hear firing to the north approximately 15 minutes after linking up, but they were still waiting on the pack train. Now I'll argue that Reno was definitely going through some post-traumatic stress (PTS) at this point and may, or may not, have been thinking clearly. By most testaments of his peers and subordinates, he did conduct himself in a very professional manner, so I believe that he never truly "lost it" but was undoubtedly shaken up. I've been on three combat tours between Iraq and Afghanistan as a door gunner on Blackhawks. I can empathize with the Major's plight. War is hell—never a more real statement said. We cannot easily judge these men on base facts only. It's too complicated a situation for such a simple summarization.

What Reno did in the meantime makes a lot of sense. He got the wounded consolidated, got his companies reorganized, got ammo redistributed from Benteen's companies, and yes, he did go looking for a fallen friend. Since Custer's instructions were to move forward with the packs, there was time available; and many things had to happen, logistically speaking.

Hearing the firing to the north Reno issued orders for the company commanders to ready the regiment to move north, and as soon as the pack train was in supporting distance, they did just that. His trek with a detachment to find Hodgson's body did not affect the timeline whatsoever—as the packs were still far to the rear, and he had already gotten all the necessary pieces moving.

Reno dispatched Hare to cut out some packs to get ammo up the hill for resupply of all the companies before the movement out and arrival of the main pack train. Reno's detractors typically never point out just how much logistics he was juggling and how it affects military actions during combat operations. Reno, with the help of Benteen, was performing well at this point.

You must also consider that during this period, Weir proceeded to move north, his company following, without orders to do so. Since this digresses from my main point, I will summarize for the sake of brevity. No meeting between Weir, Reno, and Benteen occurred as fantasized in Little Big Horn lore. Weir meant to meet with Reno and communicated this desire to Lieutenant Edgerly, but at this point, Reno was leading a detachment to try and recover Hodgson's body. It is presumed then that Weir took it upon himself to go alone forward and scout, and in seeing Weir do this, Edgerly assumed he had gotten permission and followed with the rest of the company. Weir later told Edgerly that he had not obtained permission to do so. On learning of this move, Reno immediately sent orders via Hare to Weir to contact Custer. There is no need to elaborate on Weir's movement further for this current conversation at hand. He moved to and stopped at the place we now call "Weir point." No one made it any closer to where Custer fell that day.

By the time Reno and Benteen heard firing to the north, Custer had approximately 1.5 hours of life left; and remember, no one knew that catastrophe was looming just on the horizon. Don't forget—hindsight. This firing most certainly came from either Ford B or the ridge complexes to the east, where archeology places cavalry positions. These volleys would have been the opening fighting of the Custer engagement.

From the time the first firing is heard, the packs arriving within supporting distance, a nd all of the logistics involved to move the command in place was approximately 40-50 minutes. Military logistics is not an easy task to explain or understand but are nonetheless very important. Armies do not merely move on a dime. There are always dozens, if not hundreds, of logistical items that must be taken into consideration. Reno and Benteen performed quite well in this regard.

To name a few things:

1. The wounded needed to be secured.
2. Reno's battalion needed to be reorganized.
3. Ammunition had to be cut out and dispersed.
4. Those without horses needed to be taken into account.
5. Enemies in the area needed to be kept in check.
6. Route security of the regiment and pack train must both be considered.

This was a dynamic and dangerous situation that required deliberate leadership decisions to be made. Then you have to take into account the orders for the pack train. Nothing could happen until that critical piece of logistics and intent of Custer's orders was in a position to support the regiment. It was quite a feat for all that to happen in less than an hour; once complete; Reno ordered the regiment to the north.

Now in the timeline, this places Custer arriving on or near Cemetery ridge and fighting through the basin towards battle ridge after his excursion to the Ford D area, presumably scouting a crossing at which they could threaten the non-combatants. Point of particular note: Custer's intentions during the battle are hotly contested, and I will not say with any certainty what his motivations were beyond that he was doing what he felt was necessary to accomplish the mission of the campaign. Anything he did during the battle was to serve that end. By this time, C Company had been routed, Keogh was heavily engaged in the swale, and Calhoun Hill was beginning to receive intense pressure from at least two sides. It's also at this time roughly that Weir and his company arrive in the area of Weir Point. Approximately 10-15 minutes later, Warriors began threatening the Weir Point area but were efficiently dealt with as the numbers were manageable. Ten minutes or so later, most of the regiment arrived near Weir Point.

Benteen ascended the bluffs to recon what is ahead and meets with Weir. They were utterly unable to ascertain Custer's companies' disposition and location through 2 to 3 miles of smoke and dust.

By this point, Calhoun Hill had been abandoned, Harrington's C Company had been obliterated, warriors were mopping up what's left of Keogh, and focus had shifted to the two companies left on Last Stand Hill. Within the next 15 to 20 minutes, the general fighting on the Custer battlefield would be over. Even if Reno and Benteen had kept the regiment moving forward, they could never have rescued Custer. I will also point out that the general consensus of those who were in a position to observe the Custer side of the battlefield noted that it appeared he was retreating to the north. A few even postulated that he might have been withdrawing in an attempt to link up with General Alfred Terry. The movements of Custer's companies and the flow of the fighting certainly lends some credibility to this fact as the battle more than likely flowed heavily from the south to north and this might have been the impression.

For argument's sake, had Reno left Weir Point and managed to fight through 500-1,000 warriors, there still would have been nothing left of Custer's command, and Reno, too, would have found himself fighting on the same terrible terrain as Custer did. The ground north of Reno Hill was untenable. Even Benteen said as much. That was the entire reason that Reno commanded the regiment back to Reno Hill, and within those next 15-30 minutes, most of the fighting force that had just finished with Custer turned their attention directly on Reno's command. Reno and Benteen barely escaped back to Reno Hill; if not for Godfrey's company's strategic deployment, the warriors might very well have rolled the regiment up then and there.

In conclusion, what has preceded to this point should serve to point out just how complicated things were during the battle—and even still, a great many things were summarized, paraphrased, or not mentioned due to irrelevancy to this specific dialogue. Custer's officers did not knowingly fail him; they did not abandon him to any fate by conscious choice, and they were not derelict or drunk in the execution of their duties. The continually evolving situation forced actions. Those actions held consequences for Custer, who marched his battalion out of supporting distance of his command on to ground he didn't have the numbers to keep into a situation he could not have predicted. Custer's demise boiled down to the sheer number of Sioux and Cheyenne warriors he encountered coupled with terrain that didn't favor cavalry tactics.

Appendix 3

The Kanipe Conundrum

Sergeant Daniel Kanipe, assigned to Company C of the 7th Cavalry on June 25, 1876, is a figure surrounded by much praise and also much controversy. According to Sergeant Kanipe's own volition, Captain Thomas W. Custer sent him as a messenger to the rear with the critical task of passing vital information to Captain Thomas McDougal and Lieutenant E. G. Mathey, the two men in charge of the security and movement of the pack train. The message he purportedly carried called to expedite the speed and direction of the packs. This action invariably saved his life as his company was wiped out with the rest of General George A. Custer's battalion on the day of the battle. This article's intent is not to credit nor discredit Kanipe's account of what happened that day, but rather is an exploration of the specific evidence relevant to his statements and the questions that arise from that examination.

Note: The following quotations are posted in the order they were told historically by the referenced citation.

"The firing became more distinct, and we increased our gait--a sergeant of one of the companies passed us & remarked, 'We've got them boys.' I thought all was over & that it could only have been a small village to be over so soon."
  -Edward S. Godfrey
  The Godfrey Diary

"I can't place the tepee with reference to the morass we passed, nor at what time, but just after we passed the tepee with the dead Indian in it we met a sergeant who came back going towards the pack train and he called out to some of the men in the company 'We've got 'em' leaving the inference they had captured the village."
  -Edward S. Godfrey
  Reno Court of Inquiry

Summary: Lieutenant Godfrey recalls encountering a sergeant along the march to the north (this could only have been Sergeant Kanipe) but makes no specific mention of hearing any message passed. It appears that the encounter only highlighted that the "Indians were getting whipped." A detail that led Godfrey to believe the battle will be over before they get there.

"A mile or two brought orders through a Sergeant to the officer in charge of the pack-train. I told him where I had last seen it."
  -Frederick Benteen
  Letter to wife July 1876

"A mile or so from that tepee I met a Sergeant coming back with instructions to the commanding officer of the pack train to 'Hurry up the packs', I told him the pack train I thought, was about 7 miles back and he could take the order back as I had nothing to do with that."
  -Frederick Benteen
  Reno Court of Inquiry

"A mile or so further on, I met a Sergt. Kanipe coming from the adjutant of the regiment with order----written for the commander of the pack-train. I told the sergeant the pack-train was about seven miles back, and he could take the order to the commanding officer of the pack-train to hurry up the packs, as I had nothing to do with that."
  -Frederick Benteen
  Troopers with Custer

Summary: Benteen placed a Sergeant in the area where Godfrey mentions it but only identifies him by name years after the Reno Court of Inquiry. It isn't until the later years that he says specifics such as the message coming from the "adjutant of the regiment...written for the commander of the pack-train." If "written" is to be taken literally, then it must be noted that Private Martini carried the only message that was written and passed.

"Q. Did you receive any orders during that march from the place where you received General Custer's orders till you reached Major Reno's command on the hill?

A. No, sir; the only thing was Lieut. Mathey said the engagement was going on.

Q. You received no notification to hurry up the pack train?

A. No, sir; I think Lieut. Mathey got that order - he told me about it and I told him to hurry up - I was very anxious about it."

  -Thomas McDougall

  Reno Court of Inquiry

Summary: Captain McDougall clearly states that the only correspondence he received was from Lieutenant Mathey that there was a fight going on--as also noted below. Mathey was only a lieutenant; McDougall was a captain and in overall command of the pack-train. Any order would have been passed to him to hurry the packs. The latter reference, "I think Lieut. Mathey got that order," is probably about the order that Lieutenant Hare carried to Mathey to hurry along. That is a message that is known to have been passed from Hare with Major Marcus Reno's compliments.

"Q. Who did you meet near the tepee and what orders, if any were received?

A. After passing the tepee probably two or three miles, I don' t remember the distance, I saw somebody coming back, one I remember was a half-breed and I asked him if Gen. Custer was whipping them and he said there were too many for him. I saw a great deal of smoke. When I first knew they were fighting, I stopped the head of the pack train and sent word to Capt. McDougall that they had been fighting and I would wait for him to bring up the rear. When it came up we went ahead...

Q. Did you receive orders tram General Custer or Major Reno or Capt. Benteen on that march?

A. No, sir; only such as I received from Capt. McDougall.

Q. Did any sergeant report to you with orders?

A. No, sir...

Q. Did you meet any officer there with orders?

A. After we started I met Lieut. Hare who said he wanted the ammunition and I detached two mules from the train and ordered them to go with Lieut. Hare."

  -E. G. Mathey

  Reno Court of Inquiry

Summary: Lieutenant Mathey admits to meeting someone near the vicinity where Kanipe could have been at roughly the time where he could have been there, but Mathey would never mistake Kanipe for a half-breed, so it could not have been him.

Since it can be agreed that it was Kanipe that Lieutenant Godfrey and Captain Benteen encountered along the trail, he would have more than likely also boasted to Mathey that the "Indians were getting whipped," not that there "were too many."

Mathey also clearly states that no sergeant passed any orders, and the only orders that were passed were Mathey's message to McDougall via Lieutenant Hare.

Now let's take a look at Kanipe's words and see what matches.

"I was riding close to Sergeant Finkle. We were both close to Capt. Tom Custer. Finkle hollered at me that he couldn't make it, his horse was giving out. I answered back: 'Come on, Finkle, if you can.' He dropped back a bit."

Summary: The issue here is that Kanipe cited Captain Tom Custer as being near the rear of the five companies--Company C was last in the order of the march at the time. During the battle, Captain Custer was detailed as the Aide-De-Camp to General Custer, which would place him in the Headquarters element located at the head of the column.

It is essential to note the distances involved here as well. General Custer traveled line abreast until near Reno Hill then moved into columns of four--this would place Company C and Kanipe to the far right of the line of march and a significant distance from the Headquarters element at the time and location of the message being passed.

There is also a particular conflict with this account and military logic. Since Captain Custer was detailed to the Headquarters element, it would have been highly inefficient to ride to the far right of the line to find a messenger when there were orderlies available immediately.

Another special note is that no other Company C members that survived made a note of Captain Custer passing a message or riding with the company.

"Just then the captain told me to go back and find McDougall and the pack train and deliver to them orders that had just been issued by General Custer."

Summary: The question that arises here is, when did Captain Custer receive this order from General Custer if he was back riding with his company? There is no mention of Captain Custer returning from having been with General Custer nor any mention of General Custer or Lieutenant W. W. Cooke--the assigned regimental adjutant--riding back to give him such an order.

The next logical question then is, why wouldn't General Custer or Lieutenant Cooke have passed the message personally? All messages sent up to this point came only from those two individuals. Being in no official capacity to issues orders to another battalion, Captain Custer would not have sent a message back without receiving such instructions to do so.

"'Tell McDougall,' he said, 'to bring the pack train straight across to high ground -- if packs get loose don't stop to fix them, cut them off. Come quick. Big Indian camp.'"

Summary: It's important to note that at this point of the battle, not a shot had been fired. This begs to question, why the sudden urgency now? Major Reno was still making his way down the valley, and General Custer was far to the east on the bluffs.

This brings forward the next question, why would General Custer send a messenger with similar wording twenty-something minutes later if one had already been sent? Additional messengers would be sent if there were orders contrary to or in addition to a fact. Custer sent two additional messengers during Benteen's scout to the left to further detail his previous orders, but in this case, there were no additional instructions.

If anything, the later message Martini carried was vaguer than Kanipe's, and why to Benteen to hurry up with packs and not those detailed to the pack-train's security and movement as was Kanipe's?

"I went back. I thought then that was tough luck, but it proved to be my salvation. If Sergeant Finkle had not dropped back a few minutes before he would have got the orders -- and I would not be telling this story...Reaching the pack train, I gave Captain McDougall the orders sent him, and went on toward Captain Benteen as I had been told to take them to him, also."

Summary: Lieutenant Mathey and Captain McDougall reported receiving no such message, and there is presently no testimony or accounts available which seem to contradict their testimony to this fact. It can be reasoned that Mathey and McDougall wouldn't both have forgotten such an order, and there's no motive for either of them to ignore it. Messages carry the sender's weight, so such an order would have been a direct order from the regimental commander. If received, it would have been executed as such.

Conclusion: The conundrum with Sergeant Kanipe's account is that it does not stand up well to scrutiny, and it raises more questions than there are answers. As with most things Little Big Horn, we are left with an incomplete picture of events and fragmented testimonies spread across decades. It is not my role to pass judgment on a career soldier with an otherwise good record, but it is our duty as historians and researchers to ask the hard questions.

Appendix 4

Uniforms, Weapons, Equipment and Horses of the U.S. Cavalry at the Little Big Horn

Introduction:

We are about to embark on a detailed look at the fighting men of the U.S. 7th Cavalry at the Battle of the Little Bighorn. As a soldier myself, one of the fascinating aspects of studying military history is learning the tools of my historic contemporaries' trade. This paper cannot touch on every single possible variation that existed, which there were thousands. Still, it will compile several other historians' works with that of the written record, photos, and literature for you to get a deeper understanding of how the cavalrymen went into battle that day.

General Uniforms and Equipment:

1. Uniform "blouse" jackets:

    A) 1872 style officer's blouse.

        a. Four gilt buttons and frogging on each side (the 1875 style added another button) [Douglass C. McChristian, The U.S. Army in the West, 1870 – 1880, (University of Oklahoma Press), 61].

    B) 1874 style fatigue blouse.

        a. Was current for enlisted men with five buttons and yellow cord edging on collar and cuffs [McChristian, 168].

    C) Enlisted men also wore the 1872 plaited fatigue blouse

        a. It was a style of the 1858 - 1872 long frock coat, and in many cases, was modified by being made shorter [McChristian, 62].

    D) The long-standing cavalry shell jacket.

        a. Piped in yellow for the cavalry.

    E) Sack "Saque" coat was a slightly longer, straight-sided jacket.

    F) Officer's uniform jacket, single-breasted frock coat.

        a. Company grade jackets in the 1851 – 1872 styles were single-breasted with nine gilt buttons.

        o Field grade jackets were usually double-breasted.

2. Undershirts:

    A) The standard undershirt in 1876 was gray.

        a. It was typically coarse, flannel, or knitted. In some cases, soldiers used pullover shirts.

    B) Some soldiers wore newly issued experimental dark blue shirts.

    C) Some men still wore the white shirts left over from the Civil War.

    D) Others probably wore a civilian-type, checkered "hickory" style, pink or blue shirt.

    E) Officers almost always wore the "fireman-style" blue shirt, with no rank insignia.

        a. It was double-breasted, trimmed in white tape, and usually had a set of crossed sabers with a "7" embroidered in white or yellow silk on the collar's points. [McChristian, 67 – 68]

General Note:

    a. *"(It irritated the soldier's skin) in the most excrutiating [sic] manner."*

        -Assistant Surgeon Alfred A. Woodhull

3. Overcoat "greatcoat":

    A) Light blue kersey with a long cape.

    B) Double-breasted.

    C) The 7th Cavalry pioneered a blanket-lined version as early as 1868.

    D) Only sometime after 1876 was the inside of the cape lined with the service color branch. [McChristian, 69 – 71]

General Note:

    a. *"(The men lined) their overcoats with woolen blankets…by lining the skirt of the coat they were made very comfortable as far down as the knees."*

        -First Sergeant John Ryan

4. Poncho "fish slicker":

    A) Black over wear.

    B) Tied off on the pommel when not in use per Custer's instructions.

5. Trousers:

    A) After the Civil War, the officers' trousers were changed from dark-blue, the same as their uniform coats, to the same light-blue color as the enlisted men, though of much more delicate quality material.

    B) Many officers and enlisted men reinforced their trousers with white canvas on the seat and inside legs.

    C) 1861 style officers' trousers were sky blue with a one eighth inch yellow "welt" stripe.

    D) Only officers, sergeants, and corporals were authorized to wear a trouser stripe, each of different width.

        a. Corporal – one-half inch.

        b. Sergeant – one inch.

        c. Officers - one and one-half inch.

        d. Trumpeters - double yellow stripes.

General Notes:

    a. The double stripe was not authorized until 1883, but G. A. Custer allowed it anyway. [McChristian, 61 – 64]

    b. Enlisted men wore sky-blue kersey trousers.

6. Underwear:

    A) One-piece summer weight cotton-flannel pattern.

General Note:

    a. Soldiers complained "bitterly" about old-pattern drawers. The main issue was the cut, the waist being too big and the legs being too small. Also, the crotches were known to wear out prematurely. [McChristian, 68]

7. Boots:

    A) By regulation, the trousers were supposed to cover the boot, but many ignored this on a campaign.

    B) Coarse leather and typically inferior quality.

General Note:

    a. Standard-issue boots were not quite knee-high.

8. Hats:

 A) High crowns

 B) Wide, "snap-brims," meaning sides could hook up.

 C) Trimmed with yellow worsted band and tassels.

 D) Many troops wore similar and dissimilar civilian hats because of the military-issue ones' low quality.

 E) Many C Company troopers wore gray hats. [Bruce R. Liddic, Vanishing Victory, (Upton & Sons), 143]

 General Note:

  a. Standard-issue hats were felt black.

9. Neckerchiefs:

 A) Soldiers frequently wore various styles, designs, and colors of neckerchiefs, usually based on their preference.

 General Note:

  a. Contrary to popular Hollywood belief, bulk yellow standard-issue neckerchiefs weren't a real thing.

Summary: The soldiers on the frontier in 1876 were very different than their Civil War or later contemporaries. They found themselves in a rift created by a depression that resulted from the end of the War. Much improved uniform and equipment updates were a decade overdue and a decade before they'd be genuinely relevant. In short, the fighting men on the frontier had to make the best with what they had or what they could modify.

General Uniforms and Equipment Notes:

1. *"Nearly all the men wore the blue, but many, perhaps most of them, had their trousers reinforced with white canvas on the seat and the legs from the knees half way up. Nearly everyone wore the short top boot (that was then uniform) not high like those now worn, although a few of the officers wore the Wellington boot and had white canvas leggings."*

 -Lieutenant Edward S. Godfrey

2. *"Our own moving outfit, especially as to clothing, presented very little appearance that we were United States soldiers. To a distant observer it would have been excusable to regard us as an organized horde of bandits. Only an occasional one of us had remaining on his body some article of the standard Army uniform of that period...Army hats and caps had been lost or thrown away, some substituted handkerchiefs or rags tied over heads...I settled down to wearing a calf-skin suit, of trousers and jacket...the 'hair' left on, this ordinarily worn outside. If rainy weather soaked me, at night I turned the hairy side in and slept comfortably. My underwear I hung up to dry."*

    -Private William H. White

3. *"I am unable to give a description properly of the Seventh horse as I found them on the Yellowstone River (August 2nd, 1876). Their costumes were queer ones and could not be called a uniform. Each man was dressed to his own taste with buckskin hunting shirts; blue, gray and white flannel shirts; fatigue caps, black and white campaign hats, buckskin breeches, also light blue army pattern reinforced with white canvas (flour sacking) ...the officers were dressed about the same as the men."*

    -Private Frederick H. Toby

4. *"I was dressed like most of the troopers June 25th, 1876. My hat was an Andrews style folding hat. I could see sky in several places. My shirt was the Gray issue wool. My sleeves were rolled up as it was hot that day. My faded blue coat was tied on the back on top of the grain bag. My pants were faded sky blue with numerous repairs. My boots were ruddy brown. I carried a left over Civil War Saber belt with pistol. I wore a second canvas belt to carry the Carbine Ammo. The Carbine was carried with a Civil War Carbine sling. You would not know we were Cavalry if not for the Guidons."*

    -Private William O. Taylor

5. *"It was hot that day most of the troopers had their coats tied to the back of their saddles."*

    -First Sergeant John Ryan

6. *"The hats, for the most part would have been either black or grayish white. The latter color was worn by several troops including E, C, and I believe L Company Godfrey's K Company wore white canvas pants (they were known as the 'Dude Company')."*

    -George Kush

7. *"Ninety percent of the command went into the fight in shirts, gray or blue, their jackets being on their saddles. Some non-commissioned officers who wore coats threw them off, as the marks of ranks singled them out to the Indians as chiefs. There weren't many questions asked after the battle about where the coats of those above privates went to."*

    -Private William Morris

8. *"Our officers raised their hands and gave the command 'advance.' Then came the throwing away of all surplus material, such as overcoats, hats, haversacks, etc., to make themselves as light as possible and be in fighting trim."*

    -Private John F. Donahue

<u>The Officer's Uniforms:</u>

Note: The following is based on pictorial evidence of the 1874 Yellowstone Campaign, historic manners of dress in the field, and eye witness accounts.

1. Lieutenant Colonel George A. Custer, detailed as 7th Cavalry Commander:

    A) Buckskin suit, jacket, and pants.

    B) Blue "fireman's" shirt.

    C) Piped in white; wide-brimmed, low-crowned, whitish-gray felt hat.

    D) Probably wore a red scarf.

    E) Probably had his buckskin jacket stowed on his horse because of the heat.

    General Notes:

    a. *"Custer wore a 'blue-gray flannel shirt, buckskin trousers, and long boots... a regular company hat."*

        -Trumpeter Giovani Martini

    b. *"Custer was in shirt sleeves; his buckskin pants were tucked into his boots; his buckskin shirt fastened to the rear of his saddle; and a broad-brimmed, cream colored hat... the brim of which was turned up on the right side and fastened by a small hook and eye to the crown."*

        -Private Peter Thompson

    c. *"Custer and Cooke, 'were the only ones who had blue shirts and no jackets and buckskin pants...'"*

        -Lieutenant Charles C. DeRudio

d. *"General Custer wore a broad brimmed slouch hat, buckskin shirt and pants, and high-top cavalry boots."*

    -First Sergeant John Ryan

e. *"He wore a whitish gray hat, with broad brim and rather low crown, very similar to the Cowboy hat; buck skin suit, with a fringed welt in outer seams of trousers and arms of blouse; the blouse with double-breasted military buttons, lapels generally open; turn-down collar, and fringe on bottom of shirt."*

    -Lieutenant Edward S. Godfrey

2. Captain Thomas "Tom" Custer, Headquarters, detailed as Aide-de-Camp:

A) Buckskin suit, jacket, and pants.

B) Blue "fireman's" shirt.

C) White felt hat.

General Notes:

a. Tom Custer was also known to wear a buckskin shirt.

b. *"(He) wore a broad brimmed slouch hat, a buckskin shirt..."* [Graham, 347].

c. *"Tom Custer wore regulation blue pants, but with a sergeant's stripe, not an officer's."*

    -Sergeant Daniel A. Kanipe

3. First Lieutenant William "Cookie" Cooke, Headquarters, detailed as Adjutant:

A) Buckskin suit, jacket, and pants.

B) Blue "fireman's" shirt.

C) White felt hat.

General Notes:

a. W. W. Cooke possibly wore lighter colored leather than his contemporaries.

b. *"He (Cooke) was wearing his blue shirt and buckskin pants."*

    -Lieutenant Charles C. DeRudio

4. Doctor George Lord, Surgeon, Headquarters:

A) Blue regulation shirt or possibly a "fireman's" shirt.

B) Blue regulation trousers.

C) Possibly wore glasses.

General Note:

a. Doctor Lord may have worn glasses, as in the famous "Officers and Chief Civilians of the 1874 Black Hills Expedition" pictures, as a joke.

5. Captain Myles Keogh, I Company Commander, detailed as Battalion Commander:

a) Buckskin blouse.

b) Blue "fireman's" shirt.

c) Blue regulation trousers.

d) Wore shoes rather than boots on June 25th, 1876.

General Note:

a. *"I found one of Keogh's shoes when he went with the reburial party in 1877."*

-Sergeant M. C. Caddle

6. Second Lieutenant Henry Harrington, acting C Company Commander:

A) Blue regulation blouse.

B) White canvas trousers with fringe on the outer seams.

General Note:

a. "Lieutenant Harrington wore white canvas pants with a buckskin-like fringe along the seams."

-George Kush

7. First Lieutenant James Porter, acting I Company Commander:

A) Buckskin blouse.

B) Blue "fireman's" shirt.

C) Blue regulation trousers.

General Note:

a. "I found Porter's buckskin blouse in the village… and from the shot holes in it, he must have had it on and must have been shot from the rear, left side, the bullet coming out on the left breast near the heart."

-Lieutenant Edward S. Godfrey

8. First Lieutenant James "Jimmi" Calhoun, L Company Commander:

A) Buckskin blouse.

B) Blue "fireman's" shirt.

C) Blue regulation trousers.

9. Second Lieutenant Jack Crittenden, L Company:

A) Dark blue shirt with a wide falling collar.

B) Probably wore blue regulation trousers.

C) Wore a glass eye.

10. Captain George W. Yates, F Company Commander, detailed as Battalion Commander:

A) Buckskin blouse.

B) Blue "fireman's" shirt.

C) Buckskin pants.

11. First Lieutenant Algernon Smith, E Company Commander:

A) Buckskin suit, jacket, and pants.

B) Blue vest over a white shirt.

C) Grey hat he received as a gift from George A. Custer.

D) Cavalry boots.

General Note:

a. Lieutenant Smith probably had the buckskin jacket stowed on his horse because of the heat.

b. According to Captain Thomas McDougall, *"Lieutenant Smith wore a white shirt, blue vest, buckskin pants, and cavalry boots."*

-Greg Casteel

12. Second Lieutenant James Sturgis, E Company:

A) Buckskin jacket.

B) Blue "fireman's" Shirt.

C) Blue regulation trousers.

General Notes:

a. Lieutenant Charles C. DeRudio saw a buckskin shirt with Sturgis' name on it in the Indian village. He probably removed the jacket due to the heat—the buckskin shirt could easily have been tied to his saddle or with his gear.

b. *"(Sturgis) wore his coat over his 'fireman's' shirt."*

-Lieutenant Edward S. Godfrey

13. Second Lieutenant William Van Wyck Reily, acting F Company Commander:

A) Blue "fireman's" shirt.

B) Blue regulation trousers.

14. Major Marcus Reno, Second in Command, detailed as Battalion Commander:

   A) Regulation blue undress coat.

   B) A sack or "sacque" coat.

   C) Blue regulation trousers.

   D) Straw hat.

   General Note:

   a. Reno lost his straw hat sometime between the charge down the valley and the retreat from the timber, after which he tied a red bandana around his head.

15. Second Lieutenant Benjamin 'Bennie' Hodgson, detailed as Reno's Adjutant:

   A) Dark blue shirt with a wide falling collar.

   B) Vest.

   C) Probably wore blue regulation trousers.

   General Note:

   a. *"Hodgson's watch and chain were gone, the gold bar inside his vest was still there."*

   -Sergeant Ferdinand A. Culbertson

16. First Lieutenant Charles 'Carlo' DeRudio:

   A) Dark blue shirt with a wide falling collar.

   B) Probably wore blue regulation trousers.

17. Second Lieutenant Luther Hare:

   A) Dark blue shirt with a wide falling collar.

   B) Probably wore blue regulation trousers.

18. Doctor James DeWolf, Surgeon:

   A) Probably wore the blue "fireman's" shirt.

19. Doctor Henry Porter, Assistant Surgeon:

   A) Buckskin blouse.

20. Second Lieutenant Charles Varnum, detailed as Commander of Scouts:

   A) Blue "fireman's" shirt;

   B) Probably wore a straw hat.

   C) Blue regulation trousers.

21. Captain Myles Moylan, A Company Commander:

   A) Dark blue shirt with a wide falling collar.

   B) Probably wore blue regulation trousers.

22. First Lieutenant Donald McIntosh, G Company Commander:

A) Probably wearing a buckskin shirt (It's reported he was wearing it when he was killed).

B) Probably wore blue regulation trousers.

General Note:

a. He was known to wear a buckskin coat and a blue "fireman's" shirt.

23. Second Lieutenant George Wallace, G Company:

A) Dark blue shirt with a wide falling collar.

B) Probably wore blue regulation trousers.

24. Captain Thomas French, M Company Commander:

A) Deerskin jacket.

B) Large-brimmed hat.

C) Probably wore the dark blue shirt with a wide falling collar under the jacket.

D) Probably wore blue regulation trousers.

25. Captain Frederick Benteen, H Company Commander, detailed as Battalion Commander:

A) Dark blue shirt with a wide falling collar.

B) Probably wore blue regulation trousers.

C) Probably wore an 1872 pattern campaign hat. [McChristian, 45]

26. Second Lieutenant Winfield Edgerly, D Company, detailed to Scouting Duty:

A) Blue "fireman's" shirt;

B) Black snap-brim campaign hat.

C) Probably wore blue regulation trousers.

27. Captain Thomas Weir, D Company Commander:

A) Dark blue shirt with a wide falling collar.

B) Probably wore blue regulation trousers.

28. First Lieutenant Francis 'Frank' Gibson, Acting H Company Commander:

A) Dark blue shirt with a wide falling collar.

B) Probably wore blue regulation trousers.

29. First Lieutenant Edward Godfrey, K Company Commander:

A) Dark blue shirt with a wide falling collar.

B) Probably wore blue regulation trousers.

30. Captain Thomas McDougall, B Company Commander, detailed as Battalion Commander Packtrain Security

   A) Dark blue shirt with a wide falling collar.

   B) Probably wore blue regulation trousers.

31. First Lieutenant Edward Mathey, M Company, detailed as Commander Pack Train:

   A) Dark blue shirt with a wide falling collar.

   B) Probably wore blue regulation trousers.

Summary: Within the 7th U.S. Cavalry, there existed a particular division amongst the various officers regarding how general military appearance was presented when on a campaign. There were officers of the "Custer Clan" who tended to mirror their commander and friend George A. Custer. This included wearing locally made and purchased buckskin style coats and pants. Those not within G. A. Custer's close circle typically adhered to a more professional "Army standard" look. These officers tended to mirror the more regulation appearance as prescribed by Army regulations.

The Officer's Uniforms General Notes:

1. *"All of the officers wore the dark blue shirt with rather wide falling collar, which when the blouse was worn, was over the blouse collar; most of them had cross-sabers and 7, like the old cap ornament, worked in white or yellow silk on the points of the collar."*

   -Lieutenant Edward S. Godfrey

2. *"... (T)he officers who were killed, or most all of them, wore regular soldier's uniform and I don't think that any of the officers had shoulder straps on any of their blouses. As to the wool hats I will say that 'C' Troop and 'E' and 'L' all wore white hats. The other companies of the Regiment wore black hats."*

   -Sergeant Daniel A. Kanipe

3. *"Most of the officers in Custer's battalion wore buckskin blouses, except for Harrington, Reilly, & Crittenden. G. A. Custer was said to have taken his off before the battle, but might have put it back on again once they entered action. Apparently, Tom Custer and W. W. Cooke were wearing their buckskin blouses and it is believed that the officers and non-commissioned officers (the sergeants) were expected, as a rule, to wear their blouses in combat for better identification for the troops."*

-George Kush

Summary: While the Army did have established uniform and equipment standards, it was customary for officers and soldiers in the field to modify these standards while on a campaign. Non-issue clothing, weapons, and equipment became commonplace in the 7th Cavalry. In some cases, these changes were persona-driven, such as Custer's typical "flair" look of red cravats and scarfs. Some were social style trends, such as wearing vests or "firemen shirts." Most of the individual changes were for comfort or functionality. Soldering is a tough business, so soldiers would find alternatives to make their life more comfortable or allow them to be more effective.

Standard Issue Weapons:

1. The 1873 Springfield "trapdoor" carbine was adopted in 1872 – 1873 by a military board headed by Brigadier General Alfred Terry, who examined and tested over ninety rifles for the government's pursuit of a new, post-civil war, standard-issue rifle. Ninety-nine rifles were put through rigorous tests which included: accuracy, dependability, rate-of-fire, and field survivability. The "No. 99 Springfield" was eventually selected. [Nick McGrath, "The Springfield Model 1873 Rifle," ArmyHistory.org, 2016]

   A) In service from 1873 – 1892.

   B) The carbine version fires a 405-grain lead bullet with a muzzle velocity of 1,100 feet per second.

   C) The infantry version chambers a caliber .45-70 cartridge, and the cavalry carbine version chambers a caliber .45-55 cartridge (the -70 and -55 represent the amount of black powder used in the cartridge). [McChristian, 131]

   D) The cartridge case was internally primed, copper-based, and could occasionally cause the rifle to jam when the chamber and barrel were too hot.

E) The average rate of fire is eight rounds per minute for recruits and fifteen rounds per minute for experienced soldiers.

F) Considered an excellent rifle for its time. [McGrath, 2016]

General Notes:

a. Due to the carbine's shorter barrel, the caliber 45-70 cartridge proved to have too much recoil for shooters on horseback, so the fifty-five-grain cartridge was explicitly adopted for cavalry soldiers.

b. Historically, the copper casings have been used as an argument and significant contributing factor to the Little Bighorn loss. Forensic analysis of the archeological record for cartridge casings found on the field has shown that extraction failure for split cases to be less than 2%. [Douglas D. Scott and Richard A. Fox, Archaeological Perspectives on the Battle of the Little Bighorn, (University of Oklahoma Press), 113]

2. The M1873 Colt Single Action Army (SAA) "Peacemaker" pistol was designed for U.S. Government service as part of trials conducted in 1872 for a new standard-issue military sidearm.

A) In service from 1873 – 1892.

B) Fires a 255-grain lead bullet with a forty-grain charge at a muzzle velocity of 850 feet-per-second.

C) The standard Cavalry model featured a barrel length of seven and one-half inches.

D) The casing was a brass caliber .45 Colt design.

E) The chamber could house six cartridges.

F) The average rate of fire is 180 rounds-per-minute.

General Notes:

a. Many soldiers left one chamber empty to avoid negligent discharges when riding.

b. While the rate of fire is high, the reload time is also very high. An experienced shooter could potentially reload their pistol within fifteen seconds, in good conditions. An inexperienced shooter would require significantly more time. [McChristian, 133]

Specialty Weapons:

While the average "rank and file" soldier would be carrying the 1873 Springfield rifle and the 1873 Colt revolver, the officers, scouts, and civilians typically fielded their fighting arms. The following is a list of known or possible firearms carried by specific individuals at the Little Bighorn.

1. Lieutenant Colonel George A. Custer:
    A. Carried a long barreled sporting rifle, most likely a Remington Rolling Block, probably chambered in .50-70 Government, and mostly likely used a pommel slide to secure it when mounted..
    B. Carried two pistols, purportedly of an English short barrel style, however testimonial and written evidence from John Ryan and Libbie Custer suggest that his pistols were in fact more standard arms.
    General Notes:
    a. It's still unknown exactly which rifle and pistol combo he carried into battle.
    b. *"Custer carried a Remington Sporting rifle, octagonal barrel; two 'Bulldog' self-cocking, English, white-handled pistols, with a ring in the butt for a lanyard; a hunting knife, in a beaded fringed scabbard; and a canvas cartridge belt."*
        -Lieutenant Edward S. Godfrey
    c. *"One a .45-caliber Colt, and the other a French Navy."*
        -First Sergeant John Ryan
    d. The "British Bulldog" claim made by Godfrey cannot be completely accurate as the "Bulldog" versions of these pistols weren't available until 1878. If Custer carried a pair of these, they were the 1867 Webley R.I.C. Revolvers version No 1. [Garry James, "Custer's Last Gun: Webley RIC Revolver," gunsandammo.com, 2015] [Graham, 346]

2. Captain Thomas W. Custer:
    A. Carried a long barreled sporting rifle, most likely a sporterized 1873 Springfield "Officer's Model" probably chambered in .45-70 Government.
    B. Carried a SAA Colt chambered in .45 Long Colt.
    General Note:
    a. *"...carried a .45-caliber Colt pistol, and a Springfield sporting rifle, caliber .45."* [Graham, 347].

b. The Officer's Model is an 1873 trapdoor design with a slightly longer barrel than the carbine and can feature several different "sport" modifications and graphic design elements. Such attachments were long-range "peep" sighting systems attached behind the stock's breach, which gave the shooter much more precise long-distance control.

3. Captain Thomas French:

A. Carried a .50 Caliber rifle, possibly an 1863/66 Allin conversion rifle.

General Note:

a. *"a .50, or equivalent, caliber version of the trapdoor rifle."*

-First Sergeant John Ryan

b. According to John Ryan, Captain French became agitated at some point during the fighting. In his attempts to hit distant Natives firing on their position, he eventually gave up, threw his rifle on the ground, and walked away. Ryan secured it and ended up keeping it for the rest of his life.

4. First Sergeant John Ryan:

A. Carried a 3.5x power scoped Sharps rifle chambered in either .50-70 Government or .50-90 Sharps, and was most likely a modified 1869 long range variant since Sharps did not release a new rifle model until 1874..

General Note:

a. *"a .50 caliber scoped Sharps rifle."*

-First Sergeant John Ryan

b. He would use this rifle during fighting late on June 26th to provide counter-sniper fire against Native snipers that were effectively pinning M company down from Sharpshooter Ridge.

Summary: The post-Civil War recessions had significant repercussions on the military. The reduced budget and personnel cuts left the Army in a low state of preparedness. The average allotment of ammunition per soldier was twenty rounds, and often this was used firing at the passing game. [Greg Michno, "Battle of Little Bighorn: Were the Weapons the Deciding Factor," historynet.com, 2006]

Weapons Notes:

1. Regarding the ammunition allotment per soldier, *"12 rounds per man."*

 -Captain Henry Noyes

2. Regarding the amount of ammunition each man carried into battle, *"each was issued 100 rounds..."*

 -Captain John G. Bourke

3. *"The new Springfield arms and ammunition were issued to the command today. They seem to give great satisfaction."*

 -Lieutenant James Calhoun

4. *"The Springfield 1873 Model...was a single shot cartridge gun...It would shoot and kick hard, carrying up to 500 yards very well."*

 -James Forrestell

5. *"(The Springfield rifle is) first rate...and probably the best thing that had ever been placed in the hands of troops."*

 -Colonel John Gibbon

Tack and Equipment:

The melding of man and beast is the principal foundation on which the cavalry is formed. During the post-Civil War years, the cavalry became the "go-to" units for frontier campaigns, mostly due to the nature of the Native cultures they fought.

Note: The following information is attributed to Greg Casteel, cavalry equipment expert, whereas otherwise noted.

1. The 1872 McClellan saddle:

 A) Designed by Captain George B. McClellan in 1855.

 B) Relatively unchanged since its inception.

 C) It was less expensive and light enough not to burden Cavalry horses without compromising support for the rider or equipment.

 General Note:

 a. The U.S. Cavalry equipment and tactics were heavily influenced by Russian fighting studies during the Crimean War.

b. McClellan studied tactics and equipment employed during this period for a year and later returned to the United States with over one-hundred books and manuals.

2. Saddle blanket:

A) Civil War era blue with a yellow border measuring Eighty-four by seventy-two inches.

B) Weighed approximately four pounds.

3. Bridle and halter:

A) Reins are five feet long and stitched together at the end.

4. Standard bit:

A) The bit was a curb and came in four sizes and degrees of severity.

General Note:

a. A trooper used a "snaffle," or watering bridle, for riding to water and for training and exercise.

5. Feed "nose" bag:

A) Constructed from canvas and leather.

B) Eleven inches tall by eight inches in diameter.

C) Curry comb and horse brush on the off-side ring.

6. Saddlebags:

A) Leather over-over design.

B) Approximately nine inches wide by ten inches high" and three and three-quarters inches deep with an overall length of thirty-six inches.

C) Carries a front and hind shoe, shoe nails, spare ammo, and several "odds and ends."

7. M-1872/74 Haversack:

A) Made from ten or eighteen-ounce cotton duck canvas.

B) Approximately eight and one-half inches wide by eleven inches long with two and one-half inch gusset and interior pocket.

C) Features one exterior open-top pocket (the M1874 had two additional side pockets).

D) Two-piece cotton web strap, one and one-half inches wide secured by button hooks.

E) Includes tin cup, tin plate, knife and fork (leather covers), brass candle holder, candles, matches, sewing kit, soap, razor, brush, toothbrush, Army issue coffee, playing cards, hardtack, and salt pork. [McChristian, 89 & 187]

8. M1858 (modified) or M1874 Canteen:

A) Tan outer cover.

B) Modified with triangle loops.

C) Adjustable leather sling with brass hooks. [McChristian, 210]

9. Rolled blanket on the cantle

A) Standard issue wool.

10. Picket pin and lariat:

A) Per G. A. Custer, coiled on the front nearside ring.

11. Pommel slide:

A) Became very popular amongst the seventh cavalry troops.

B) Allows the rifle to be mounted parallel to the ground and perpendicular to the rider via the pommel to keep control of it.

C) Allows for expedient retrieval and stowing of soldier's rifles.

12. Carbine sling:

A) The carbine was carried on the right side, suspended on a broad leather strap resting on the left shoulder.

B) The muzzle pointed down when dismounted, and when mounted, the barrel was loosely held by a leather socket near the saddle stirrup. The use of a pommel slide typically rendered the carbine sling obsolete to the user.

13. Ammo carrying equipment "Prairie Belts":

A) M1876 cartridge belt "Fair-Weather Christian cartridge belt."

B) Prairie cartridge belt (tan webbing with black leather).

C) M1874 45/70 Mc Keever cartridge box.

D) M1874 45/70 Dyer cartridge pouch.

E) M1874 pistol cartridge pouch.

General Note:

a. Prairie belts and other ammo carrying items were typically locally made from existing standard-issue items. [McChristian, 216-221]

Summary: In the post-Civil War years, it took some time for the military to catch up to the soldiers' needs in the field. Most of the issue items were leftovers from the Civil War; in most cases, only simple updates and modifications were made before issuing them to the line units. The military supply problem stemmed from a massive recession due to the cost of the Civil War and a fractured trade market. The lower quality, and often the lack of effectiveness, typically forced officers and enlisted men to procure suitable replacements from the local Sutler. Numerous and creative modifications were frequently made to make campaign life either more comfortable or enhance one's effectiveness at Soldiering.

Horses of a Different Color:

Per G. A. Custer, the seventh cavalry adopted a horse coloring scheme to the disposition of horses across the regiment. This "color coding" assisted men and commanders in identifying units on the field of battle. There were several variations within each company. The color coordination of horses or "troop designation" was a long-standing tradition in European armies before the U.S. Civil War. [Custer Lives, A Horse of a Different Color] [First Sergeant John Ryan, Company M, Seventh Cavalry]

1. Horse colors by the company:
    A) A Company's color scheme centered on Black Horses and was a mixture of Ravens and Coals.
    B) B Company's color scheme centered on light Bay horses and was a mixture of Duns and Buckskins.
    C) C Company's color scheme centered on light Sorrel horses and was a mixture of Bright Sorrels, Blonde Sorrels, light Chestnuts, and Palominos.
    D) D Company's color scheme centered on dark Bay horses ad was a mixture of dark Sorrels, Liver Chestnuts, dark Chestnuts, Seal Browns, and some Blacks.
    E) E Company's color scheme centered on Gray horses with possibly a few white horses and was known as the "Gray Horse Troop."
    F) F Company's color scheme centered on standard Bay horses and was a mixture of Mahogany Bays, Blood Bays, standard Chestnuts, and standard Browns.
    G) G Company's color scheme centered on light Bay horses: a mixture of Duns

and Buckskins.

H) H Company's color scheme centered on light Bay horses: a mixture of Duns and Buckskins.

I) I Company's color scheme centered on standard Bay horses and was a mixture of Mahogany Bays, Blood Bays, standard Chestnuts, and standard Browns.

J) K Company's color scheme centered on standard Sorrels and was a mixture of Chestnut Sorrels, bright Chestnuts, and dusty Chestnuts.

K) L Company's color scheme centered on standard Bay horses and was a mixture of Mahogany Bays, Blood Bays, standard Chestnuts, and standard Browns.

L) M company was a mixed horse color company and was a mixture of Copper Duns, Grulla Duns, Red Roan Bays, Rose Grey Chestnuts, Claybank Chestnuts, young Grays, paint, Blacks, and any other mixed color breeds.

Officer's Horses:

1. Lieutenant Colonel George A. Custer rode his horse "Vic." It was a Kentucky Sorrel with three white stockings and a white face. [Private John W. Burkman, Company L, Seventh Cavalry] [Hardorff, 120]

2. Captain Thomas W. Custer rode a Sorrel Gelding named "Bombshell."

3. Captain Miles Keogh rode a bay horse named "Comanche."

4. Captain Myles Moylan rode a black Gelding.

5. Captain Thomas Weir rode a black Gelding.

6. Lieutenant Benjamin Harrington rode a Sorrel Gelding.

7. Lieutenant Algernon Smith rode his black Gelding.

8. Lieutenant James Sturgis rode a Bay horse.

9. Lieutenant James Calhoun rode a white horse.

10. Lieutenant William W. Cooke rode a white horse.

General Horse Notes:

1. *"Both men and horses were in excellent condition when they set out on the 2 Second."*
   -Lieutenant E. Maguire

2. *"… [W]e weren't anywheres near being worn out… our mounts were doing fairly well. Most of them were strong young cavalry horses."*
   -Private Charles A. Windolph

3. Private William Slaper claimed that the forced night march accounted for *"the worn condition of our horses during the battle...."*

    -Private William Slaper

4. Gerard did not notice any fatigue in the troops' horses. He felt his own was reasonably fresh and he stated he could ride him *"40 or 50 miles the next day."* He had no grain, however, for his horse.

    -Fred Gerard

5. *"Our horses were beginning to wear out, many of them straggling to the rear."*

    -Lieutenant Edward S. Godfrey

6. *"Their horses were 'jaded.'"*

    -Lieutenant Francis Gibson

7. *"The horses were not tired and the troops were in great spirits."*

    -George Herendeen, Scout

8. *"The horses were in pretty good condition, many wanting to run."*

    -Doctor Henry Porter

9. *"Vic (Custer's horse) was killed; Dandy (Custer's horse in reserve) was with pack train."*

    -Lieutenant Winfield Edgerly

Summary: The consensus is that the horses went into battle without being rested, perhaps even watered. Like a person, each horse would have its limit it could reach. This is evident by the soldiers whose horses broke down on Custer's dash to get around the village, while the rest of the command seemed to move on fine at such a gait. The limit of man and horse was invariably tested those two long days in June of 1876.

Bibliography

Barnard, Sandy. Ten Years With Custer, (AST Press). May 31, 2001.

Bradley, James H. The March of the Montana Column, (University of Oklahoma Press), 1961.

Brinstool, E. A. Fighting Indian Warriors, (Indian Head Books), 1953.

Brinstool, E. A. Troopers with Custer, (Stackpole Books), 1952.

Camp,Walter. Custer in '76, (University of Oklahoma Press), 1976.

Casteel, Greg. Historian and reenactor, Online Forums or History Group Topic Discussions.

Connell, Evan S. Son of the Morning Star, (North Point Press), 1984.

Cox, Kurt H. Custer and His Commands - From West Point to Little Bighorn, (Pen & Sword Military), 2015.

Donahue, Michael N. Where the Rivers Ran Red, (San Juan Publishing), 2018.

Donahue, Michael N. Drawing Battle Lines – The Map Testimony of Custer's Last Fight, (Upton & Sons), 2008.

Donovan, James A. A Terrible Glory: Custer and the Little Bighorn, ((Little, Brown, and Company), 2008.

Fox, Richard A. Archeology, History, and Custer's Last Battle, (University of Oklahoma Press), 1993

Godfrey, Edward S. The Godfrey Diary, (Champoed Press), 1957.

Graham, William A. The Custer Myth, (Stackpole Books), 2017.

Gray, John S. Custer's Last Campaign, (University of Nebraska Press), 1991.

Hanson, Joseph M. The Conquest of the Missouri, (Stackpole Books). 2003.

Hardorff and Camp, Camp, Custer, and the Little Bighorn, (Upton & Sons). 1997.

Hardorff and Camp, On the Little Bighorn With Walter Camp 1865-1925: A Collection of W. M. Camp's Letters, Notes and Opinions on Custer's Last Fight, (Upton & Sons). 2002.

Hardorff, Richard G. The Custer Battle Casualties, (Upton & Sons), 1989.

Hardorff, Richard G. The Custer Battle Casualties II, (Upton & Sons), 1999.

Individual Quotes by, COL John Gibbon, Montana Column Commander; CPT Frederick Benteen, Company H, Seventh Cavalry; CPT Thomas McDougall, Company B, Seventh Cavalry; LT Edward S. Godfrey, Company K, Seventh Cavalry; LT Charles C. DeRudio, Company E, Seventh Cavalry; LT E. McClernand, Second Cavalry; LT Luther Hare, Company K, Seventh Cavalry; LT Francis Gibson, Company D, Seventh Cavalry; LT Winfield Edgerly, Company D, Seventh Cavalry; LT James Calhoun, Company L, Seventh Cavalry; LT E. Maguire, Engineer Officer; Henry Porter, Doctor, Seventh Cavalry; 1SG John Ryan, Company M, Seventh Cavalry; SGT Daniel A. Kanipe, Company C, Seventh Cavalry; SGT Ferdinand A. Culbertson, Company A, Seventh Cavalry; Trumpeter William Hardy, Company A, Seventh Cavalry; Trumpeter Giovani Martini, Company H, Seventh Cavalry; Private Edward H. Pickard, Company F, Seventh Cavalry; Private William H. White, Company F, Second Cavalry; Private Frederick H. Toby, Company L, Seventh Cavalry; Private William O. Taylor, Company A, Seventh Cavalry; Private John F. Donahue, Company K, Seventh Cavalry; Private Peter Thompson, Company C, Seventh Cavalry; Private Charles A. Windolph, Company H, Seventh Cavalry; Private William Slaper, Company M, Seventh Cavalry; Private Jacob Adams, Company H, Seventh Cavalry; George Herendeen, Scout, Seventh Cavalry; Fred Gerard, Interpreter, Seventh Cavalry.

James, Garry. "Custer's Last Gun: Webley RIC Revolver," gunsandammo.com. 2015.

Kush, George, Author and historian, Online Forums or History Group Topic Discussions.

Liddic, Bruce R. Vanishing Victory, (Upton & Sons), November 30, 2004.

Lundin, Scott. Historian and researcher, Online Forums or History Group Topic Discussions.

McChristian, Douglass C. The U.S. Army in the West, 1870 – 1880, (University of Oklahoma Press), March 6, 2006.

McGrath, Nick. "The Springfield Model 1873 Rifle," ArmyHistory.org. September 9, 2016.

Michno, Greg. "Battle of Little Bighorn: Were the Weapons the Deciding Factor," historynet.com. 2006.

Michno, Greg. Lakota Noon, (Mountain Press Publishing), 1997.

Michno, Greg, Author and historian, Online Forums or History Group Topic Discussions.

Nichols, Ronald H. Reno Court of Inquiry, Proceedings of a Court of Inquiry in the Case of Major Marcus A. Reno, (Custer Battlefield Historical & Museum Assoc). 1992.

Nichols, Ronald H. Men With Custer, (Custer Battlefield Historical & Museum Assoc). 2010.

Rankin, Charles E. Legacy - New Perspectives on the Battle of the Little Bighorn, (Montana Historical Society Press), 1996.

Rini, Bill. Historian and researcher, Online Forums or History Group Topic Discussions.

Scott and Fox, Archaeological Perspectives on the Battle of the Little Bighorn, (University of Oklahoma Press). June 1, 1989.

Stevenson, Joan N. Deliverance from the Little Bighorn - Doctor Henry Porter and Custer's Seventh Cavalry, (of Oklahoma Press), 2012.

Taylor, W. O. With Custer on the Little Bighorn, (Penguin Books), 2004.

Thomas, Colonel Rodney G. Rubbing Out Long Hair - The American Indian Story of the Little Big Horn in Art and Word, (Elk Plain Press), 2009.

Upton, Richard. Custer Catastrophe at the Little Bighorn 1876, (Upton & Sons), 2012.

Urwin, Gregory. Custer Victorious, (University of Nebraska Press), 1990.

Utley, Robert M. Little Bighorn Battlefield – A History and Guide to the Battle of the Little Bighorn, (National Park Service), 1994.

Vaughn, J. W. With Crook at the Rosebud, (Independently published). November 3, 2016.

Wagner, Frederic C. Participants in the Battle of the Little Big Horn - A Biographical Dictionary of Sioux, Cheyenne, and United States Military Personnel, (McFarland), 2016.

Wagner, Frederic C. The Strategy of Defeat at the Little Big Horn, (McFarland), 2014.

Wagner, Frederic C. Author and historian, Online Forums or History Group Topic Discussions.

Windolph, Charles. I Fought with Custer, (Bison Books). September 1, 1987.

Worman, Charles G. Gunsmoke and Saddle Leather, (University of New Mexico Press), 541.

About the Author

Chris Hoffert is an Army combat veteran with over twenty years of personal study and research on the Little Big Horn battle and is an award-winning director with over 15 years of film experience. He is also a Custer Battlefield Preservation Committee lifetime member and maintains membership with the Little Big Horn Associates. Chris frequently engages with other authors, historians, and battle students online to keep history relevant and alive while furthering more in-depth discussions into one of the most ambiguous battles of all time. Serving as the videographer for the U.S. Cavalry School for over seven years, Chris is heavily entangled in the Little Big Horn history. He spends several weeks each year at the battlefield with period reenactors conducting filming designed to bring history to life in a way that books simply cannot.

Chris's digital animations, 3D terrain analysis, and film work on the battle are designed to help usher historical research into the modern era by allowing students of the battle the ability to see things in a way that has never been done before. This interest in animation and 3D design began while working on the documentary 'Contested Ground' where Chris created moving maps of the entire battle to accompany the narrative video. This has since progressed into timeline analysis videos and full 3D modeling of the battlefield. Chris graduated Cum Laude from the Academy of Art University, receiving a B.F.A. and an A.A. in motion pictures and television. David Worth, a Hollywood director, author, and professor heralded Chris as "The Sergio Leone of Montana" for his ability to churn out quality gritty period films on micro-budgets.

www.chrishoffertfilm.com

Made in the USA
Monee, IL
27 March 2021

64042464R10083